The Choice is Yours

TAKE BACK THE REINS

The Truth About Why You're Stuck and How to Get Moving Again

Hallie Bigliardi

Hallie Byp

Take Back the Reins: The Truth About Why You're Stuck and How to Get Moving Again
By Hallie Bigliardi

Published by Kairos Publishing House
San Jose, CA

Publisher's Cataloging-in-Publication data

Names: Bigliardi, Hallie, author.
Title: Take back the reins : the truth about why you're stuck and how to get moving again
/ Hallie Bigliardi.
Description: First trade paperback original edition. | San Jose [California] : Kairos Publishing House, 2018. Also being published as an ebook.
Identifiers: ISBN 978-0-692-12917-3
Subjects: LCSH: Self-help techniques. | Spiritual healing. | Spiritual life— Handbooks, manuals, etc.
BISAC: SELF-HELP / Transformation.
Classification: LCC BF636 2018 | DDC 158–dc23

Cover and Interior design by Nick Zelinger, NZGraphics.com
Cover photography by Cameron Ashley Smith

QUANTITY PURCHASES: Schools, companies, professional groups, clubs, and other organizations may qualify for special terms when ordering quantities of this title. For information, email Hallie@HallieBigliardi.com.

This book is printed in the United States of America.

This book is dedicated to Kali, Michaella, and Achille,
three uniquely beautiful souls who have given me
the opportunity to be their mother. May their
lives be full of love and possibility,
and may they shine brightly.

CONTENTS

FOREWORD

Wow. What can I say about Hallie?

Hallie Bigliardi has studied SkyHorse Equine Guided Education with me since 2010 and has completed fifteen of my SkyHorse EGE™ certification programs. She is sincere, honest, kind and full-hearted, and a grounded presence. She is a rock. And she gets it. She has been a dedicated student, trusted colleague, and has become a dear friend and an amazing Equine Guided Educator.

One of the many things I love about Hallie is that she leaves no stone unturned, and yet she listens with amazing patience; she is like a meandering stream offering a quiet place for reflection to find yourself in your own mirror. She embodies EGE as a way of being—a way of being present, with the fine-tuned skill of listening deeply and without judgment "just like a horse" and the coaching skills to know when to allow those quiet spaces and when to offer astute observations gleaned from years of training.

When I first met Hallie, she knew she wanted a change. Besides being an amazing mother of three and a dedicated wife, she wanted her own identity, her own sense of purpose and contribution. She had a passion for horses and helping people. She followed her intuition to one of my Equine Guided Coaching programs and thus began her journey of becoming a SkyHorse Equine Guided Educator.

At first she was unsure of herself because she had no coach training background. We looked at some coaching programs, but nothing really fit the unique application of horses in human growth and learning. I assured her if she studied with me and the horses, she would gain not only the coaching skills to be a successful coach and facilitator, she would gain the very specific and unique skills required to do Equine

Guided Coaching. After all, I had co-founded the Strozzi Institute (Center for Leadership & Mastery) and had been training somatic coaches since 1994.

Equine Guided Coaching not only incorporates my unique approach to Somatics, it incorporates my lifetime experience as a zoologist, wildlife rehabilitator, horse trainer, leadership coach, and environmentalist.

I am so honored to write this forward for Hallie's book because she has written an eloquent, easy to follow guide to inspire you to begin your journey into *Taking Back the Reins*. No room for being stuck anymore! Simply put, no reason to. Hallie leads the way, showing you that you are your own maker. You are the designer and fulfiller of your life. No one else.

Read this book, and you will be riveted with one Aha! after another. And, if you are interested in SkyHorse EGE™ in particular, Hallie offers well-researched concepts that comprise parts of EGE, as well as several case studies gained from her years of experience.

Today, Equine Guided coaches no longer have to explain, *Why Horses?*, like I used to for so many years. There is now so much evidence grounded in science that wasn't present when I started out. I am pleased that Hallie sought out this research, which she includes in this book, to further ground why and how EGE works. From my experience, Equine Guided Education is the quickest, most thorough method of "getting unstuck" and getting re-connected with who you are and how you want to be seen in the world. With the guidance of qualified and gifted facilitators like Hallie, it also offers exercises and practices to let go of those "old stories" that are no longer serving you, and position you to walk into your new life with purpose and passion. Synchronicity and all the support you could ever imagine will find you at this crossroads, as what you dream of becomes reality.

Hallie knows this from experience. She took the reins in her hands, she did the hard work of uncovering old concepts and assumptions that no longer served her. She trained and studied the skills she needed to become the person she truly wanted to be. I admire Hallie. I honor and cherish her. I know you will find this book full of insights to help get you unstuck and on the path to being honestly and authentically yourself. It's time to set yourself free, start now with Hallie's book. I look forward to seeing your star shine in the amazing, magical, and mysterious world of the energy of being.

Ariana Strozzi Mazzucchi
Earthwhisperer.net

INTRODUCTION

Since age eight, I've felt drawn to horses. Standing on the backyard fence boards, I would stretch out my hand to offer a sugar cube to the neighbor's horse, hoping he would come closer, and I might get to touch his velvety coat. My tenth birthday present was horse camp where I learned to ride. From there my passion for horses was fixed, and I began to fantasize about a career working with them.

As a young girl, I also made a habit of studying the adults around me. At family parties and other gatherings, I would try to sit next to the adult table, so I could listen in on their conversations. I was much more interested in what they were saying than playing with kids my own age. I wanted to understand things from their perspectives. If the topic of conversation was sensitive, they would often speak in "code" to disguise the specific circumstances and identity of the people they were talking about from me and the other children. It became a game for me to listen to their conversations and try to figure out who they were talking about, to understand the problem, and guess what they thought the solution might be before they said it. I learned to listen for clues and look for patterns.

It's uncanny how these two seemingly unrelated passions could come together and culminate into work that helps other people while being both inspirational and satisfying for me. At my core, I am inspired by horses, and I'm passionate about human development and helping people discover how to get unstuck, remove barriers, and overcome the obstacles that keep us from reaching our full potential and living a fulfilling life.

When people ask me what I do for work, I wish I could reply with a quick one or two words to describe it. My official title doesn't exactly roll off the tongue: SkyHorseEGE™ Certified Equine Guided Coach and Instructor, and to say I'm a coach doesn't really tell the story of what I do. For brevity's sake, that's usually what I say, but really, I'm more of a human development detective working to decipher the clues to life's riddles.

And I've been doing it most of my life. In addition to learning through studying adult themes as a child, many lessons of adulthood came to me through my personal experiences of marriage, divorce, single parenthood, remarriage to the same man, and changing careers, among other challenging and momentous life events.

As life brought me more human development lessons, the horse-driven part of me continued to evolve. Around the time I bought my first horse, at age thirty, I thought I wanted to learn to train horses. At my riding instructor's suggestion, I bought a beautiful, copper-penny chestnut, off-the-track thoroughbred mare. She was five years old and still quite green. Within the first six months of working with her, due to my lack of training experience, I got kicked in the ribs and bucked off. These serious injuries helped me decide not to pursue horse training, and I sent her to a professional trainer.

In my mid-thirties, it occurred to me that perhaps it was time to put away my childish love of horses. As a mother with three young children, I wondered if it was irresponsible and selfish of me to be hiring a babysitter so I could go spend time at the barn with my horse.

Around the same time I began to consider giving up horses in my life, I was hit with some health challenges that pushed me to further examine who I was, what was important to me, and who I wished to become. In 2010, during this period of self-examination, I was introduced to SkyHorse Equine Guided Education™ (EGE), an experiential learning program that incorporates horses into human development. This opportunity to improve myself and develop my awareness and intuition while being around horses was the best thing I'd ever heard of, so I signed up.

When I entered the SkyHorseEGE™ certification program, I was there for my own learning and self-development, as well as my curiosity and interest in how horses could help people with their human development challenges. I did not have a plan for a professional EGE career, but as it was a training course, the program included opportunities to practice facilitating and leading sessions, and I found the EGE work came naturally to me. Following my certification, I continued to study under Ariana Strozzi Mazzucchi, the founder of SkyHorseEGE™, and I staffed for many of her courses and workshops. It became clear that horses would remain a part of my life.

Less than a year later, I had an experience that confirmed my calling to the work of EGE. I was assisting Ariana during a certification course when she asked me to take over the class. I'd led exercises before, but this was the first time she left me alone to teach. I entered the arena with the horses and faced the group of students standing just outside along the fence. I led the group into an exercise on being present and increasing self-awareness. As I led, a sorrel mare named Cowgirl came over and stood on my left side, about two feet away, and also faced the group. I introduced Cowgirl to them and expressed my appreciation for her presence, noting that her position suggested she was supporting me.

We continued the exercise and a few moments later Cowgirl lay down next to me. It is not unusual in EGE work to see the horses lie down, but I'd never had a horse lie down right next to me like that before or since. In that moment I felt connected to myself, without self-consciousness. I felt connected to the horses and the group, and I felt a sense of grounded confidence that I was exactly where I belonged. It was as if Cowgirl was an ambassador for the herd and the group, and her action was a symbolic acknowledgment of their trust in my leadership. The support and trust of the horses and humans was palpable, and in that moment I knew that EGE was part of me and I was part of it.

Since that day, I have worked with hundreds of people who wanted to get unstuck or make changes in their lives. I've developed my own unique approach to incorporating EGE and other human development concepts and methods to help me and my clients move through change and challenging transitions. As a result of their EGE experience, the clients I've worked with report greater career satisfaction, better health, reduction and elimination of pain, improved relationships, reduced anxiety, and increased clarity of purpose.

In this book, I share my views on human development and the way humans are wired. As you read, perhaps you will begin to see yourself in a new way and gain a new awareness that will lead you to possibilities and opportunities that you did not see before. If you're feeling stuck, I hope you will find new perspectives and clues that help you identify what's holding you back and blocking you from reaching your highest potential. With new awareness, you can make new choices and move toward the life you want.

I've included client stories and my own stories to help illustrate the aspects of who we are as human beings, the challenges we all face, what keeps us stuck, and how to get unstuck. Some of these stories also show how the horses guide us to find the insights and answers that are already inside of us.

Within a person's story, their history, their circumstances, and their reactions are clues or "bread crumbs" for solving life's riddles. I use psychological distinctions, somatic awareness, human development cycles, archetypal patterns, the energetics of communication, and more to identify the clues.

Problems are like puzzles to me, and if I am persistent, while remaining open and curious, I know the missing piece will emerge to help me facilitate my clients toward their own discovery. I don't solve problems for people. I facilitate people to solve their own problems. Sometimes I coach with specific guidance but mostly my work is about asking the right questions. And getting to the right question comes from following the clues, having a sense of curiosity, and a belief that there is always a solution. I see problems like a prism; they have multiple windows or faces. If I don't see what I need through one window, I change my perspective and look at it from another angle. And through EGE, the horse offers clues that I could not find any other way.

The goal of my work and the purpose behind writing this book is to guide you toward uncovering what's keeping you stuck, so you can experience a breakthrough, allowing you the freedom to be your authentic self and live a life that resonates with your whole being—mind, body, spirit, and soul.

As you read through the pages, notice what catches your attention. Take notes on the things you relate to and take special note of anything I say that you find irritating. Sometimes the things that irritate us are the best clues to help uncover what's keeping us stuck and holding us back. Review your notes and re-read the parts that stood out to you. If you let go of any judgment and do this with a sense of openness to new information, there's a good chance you'll find a clue or a new perspective that will help you take back the reins and move toward flow and satisfaction.

PART 1:
What Keeps You Stuck

1

Stuck and It Sucks

"I'm stuck, and it sucks!" How many times have we thought that? No one likes being stuck. No one likes feeling the frustration. Sometimes being stuck slows us down as we move toward a goal; other times it can stop us in our tracks. In some cases, it's annoying, in others it's a matter of life and death.

When Natalie came for her Equine Guided Education session with Cari (the horse) and me, she was worried about her daughter's safety, as well as her own. A few years earlier, Natalie had been a single mom longing for a relationship, but with her busy work schedule and taking care of her daughter, she didn't have many opportunities to meet men. One day, Natalie stayed home from work to accept a delivery of new furniture. She was surprised to find herself attracted to the man who delivered it. They struck up a friendly conversation, and before he left he asked Natalie out on a date. Their romance blossomed, and a year later they were married.

After a year of marriage, with the stability of two incomes, Natalie used her savings for the down payment on a house. Life was great … for a while.

As time moved on, Natalie's husband, Bob, began to assert himself in the discipline of her daughter, Paige. Bob's way of disciplining was harsher than hers, but Natalie figured it was normal for a mom to be softer, and she was glad that Bob was participating in parenting, even though he was a new stepfather. It was important to Natalie for Paige to have a father figure in her life.

One morning, twelve-year-old Paige made breakfast for herself. She used the last of the butter on the butter dish, so she added a new stick. Bob was furious because Paige had not washed the dish before adding new butter, and he spanked her with a belt.

Natalie felt Bob's punishment was excessive. When she tried to talk to him about it, he became defensive and aggressive. Natalie started to become concerned for her daughter and the impact of Bob's harshness. Then, Natalie started noticing other things about Bob's behavior that worried her, like his possessiveness and the fact that he was always checking up on her. But Natalie loved Bob, and she was happy to be in a relationship with him. They had a nice life together and a beautiful home, something she never thought she could have on her own.

A few weeks went by, and something horrible happened. One of Bob's motorcycle friends was dead. He had killed his wife, and after being chased by the police, he used the gun on himself. This situation alarmed Natalie. She knew that Bob was a gun collector. He had a safe full of handguns and rifles. Would Bob be capable of the same violence?

Natalie started to question. Who was this man she had married? They had only dated for a year. And what about his friends? The man who had killed his wife was one of Bob's closest friends. If the people he hung out with were capable of this type of violence, what did that say about Bob?

Natalie began to fear for her safety and her daughter's. She didn't know what to do. If she tried to leave Bob, it would make him angry, and if he truly were dangerous, what would he do to her or Paige? And what about the house? All her money had gone into the down payment. How would she get it back? And where would she go ... where *could* she go to be safe from this guy?

"But wait!" she wondered. Maybe she was blowing this all out of proportion. Maybe she was overreacting. It probably was not as bad as she was making it out to be. Natalie's thoughts swirled. Her rational mind was trying to talk her out of her intuitive fear. Her rational mind was pointing to the financial and logistical challenges of leaving Bob. It would involve such a big change; it would upend her entire life. "This situation is not *that* bad; it doesn't call for such drastic measures," her mind would say. And at the same time, her intuition kept insisting "You and Paige are not safe. You need to do something." Her conflicting thoughts went around and around.

Natalie wasn't sure which part of herself she should listen to. The fact she had allowed herself to get into this relationship in the first place caused her to doubt her judgment. She did not trust her internal sense of what to do, but placating her logical mind was not taking away the fear.

Natalie was stuck. She felt trapped, confused, and afraid.

When Natalie entered the round pen, Cari came right up to greet her. Cari stood near as Natalie spoke from her heart, sharing her concerns for her daughter and herself. Natalie confessed that she had lost trust in herself.

"Cari doesn't always walk right up to someone and stand with them," I said. "Cari trusts you, or she would not do this." I also noted the way Cari was standing, and I asked Natalie what she thought about it.

"Cari is standing tall. She looks strong and powerful," Natalie replied. I invited Natalie to stand the way Cari was standing. She did, and right away, something shifted. Natalie felt her own strength. Cari reflected to Natalie who she was on the inside, before the fear and the self-doubt had eaten away at her confidence. This led Natalie to conclude that if the horse could trust her, then she could trust herself.

Through her experience with Cari, Natalie regained her trust in herself and her ability to accurately perceive the level of danger she was in. She was not safe, and she needed to make a change.

The next day, I got an email from Natalie thanking me for the session. She wrote, "I can't describe how I feel, but suffice it to say that I know I have the strength and courage to take the next step in my life and close this chapter. I have to take one step at a time, patiently setting all the wheels in motion and make this a safe departure. Thank you! Today has been a peaceful day."

Over the next few months, Natalie made secret plans, and then one morning, she left the house giving her husband the impression she was following her normal routine: to drop Paige off at school before going to work. But instead of driving to the school, Natalie and Paige went to the airport and fled to Australia where Natalie's family lives. As of this writing, both are safe and living happily without any fear of Bob.

In Natalie's case, getting unstuck was a matter of life and death, but being stuck isn't always a matter of physical safety. More often, our stuckness causes a gradual seeping away of our life force, vitality, and the zest of living life fully. In our younger years, with a lot of life still in front of us, this may not seem so pressing. But for Marlene, a woman in her mid-sixties, getting unstuck became urgent in a different way.

Marlene and I first worked together over the course of a week-long group workshop organized by my mentor, Ariana Strozzi Mazzucchi, the one who coined the term *Equine Guided Education* and the founder of SkyHorseEGE™. On the first day, Marlene shared that she had been a clergywoman for the past eighteen years, and over the last couple she had begun thinking of retirement. "What I want is some courage to redefine my sense of confidence," she said. Growing up, Marlene's family's credo was to put on a good face and present your best. With an abusive father and an alcoholic mother, Marlene took on the responsibility of holding things together and hiding the family's flaws.

As a young girl, Marlene acted out of perceived obligations to her family and what she thought she *should* do. She had become stuck in a pattern of putting everyone else's needs ahead of her own. Between third and seventh grade, she hardly went to school because she was home taking care of her intoxicated mother. This pattern continued into adulthood. Each time she would make a decision based on her own needs, she would backtrack, worrying about how others would respond or feel, and then she would feel stuck.

"I don't know what it means to have choices," she told the group.

Two steps forward and two steps back is no way to make progress, yet this was Marlene's pattern when she first worked with Lily in the round pen. In this EGE exercise, Marlene had the opportunity to practice moving forward toward her goals by inviting Lily to walk forward with her. As Marlene spoke to Lily about the life she wanted, Marlene would take two steps forward toward her goal, and then she would turn away and walk back to where she began. Marlene then started again and repeated the same pattern. Lily's feet never moved.

At this time, Ariana was facilitating, and she asked, "Why do you stop and turn away from where you are going? Is there someone you are worried about?"

Marlene took a deep breath and shared that she felt fear, the fear of being as alone on the outside as she felt on the inside. Marlene felt alone on the inside because she had abandoned herself by making her own needs less important than everyone else's. And she was afraid that if she made her own needs the priority the people in her life would abandon her, making her feel alone on the outside too. Marlene was able to see that her desire to retire from the clergy was connected to a desire to take care of herself first, and this triggered her fear.

In her final session of the week, Marlene had another opportunity to work in the round pen with Lily, and this time, I was her facilitator. A dense fog surrounded us, and the air was full of mist. From the center of the pen, Marlene reflected on her EGE exercise from the day before when she had worked with a palomino horse named Sky. As Marlene spoke, Lily stood next to her gently nibbling on the grass. "My declaration yesterday, while leading Sky, was about discovering and acting on what is best for me. I want to embody that. I think this is about standing my ground."

Marlene continued, "I'm used to basing my comfort on everyone else's comfort. Before I can make a decision, I have to ask, 'Is this okay?' or I put it off." Lily began to move around the pen. "I want to retire," Marlene declared. "And I'll be modeling something in how I do it." This phrase caught Marlene's breath. She felt her heart rate increase. I noticed Lily's movement increase. Marlene held her chest, fighting for a deeper breath. "I want to leave, and I need to know that it's okay that I do it." Marlene caught herself, "I've already planned it out before I've really told anybody what I'm doing."

Lily, a confident and usually calm mare, began to pace the fence inside the round pen. Back and forth she walked. She was looking out, occasionally letting out a loud whinny. Marlene followed Lily. They walked together, back and forth and around. Looking out of the pen. "What is happening for you?" I asked. A few more moments passed. Their pacing continued.

Then Lily's pace increased. She began to trot. Marlene stood still and watched her. Back and forth, Lily trotted looking out beyond the fence. Lily's whinnies increased in frequency and became shrill, piercing the morning air. Lily looked out. She cried out, trotting back and forth.

Marlene finally spoke, "Lily is acting out my accumulated years of working at Calvary, and the pain I've been bearing, and how it's time for me to get out beyond Calvary. She is looking out over the fence, and she needs to be set free. She is agitated. When she whinnies, she is reflecting me and saying, 'Is there anyone out there who realizes how I'm feeling? There is so much pain. I need to get out.'" Marlene took a deep breath. Lily slowed to a walk, but continued pacing.

"I need to let myself out," Marlene said with a sigh. "Can I let Lily out of the pen?" she asked.

"That would be a great metaphor," I replied, "but not yet. Lily has more to show you."

Lily continued to walk around and around, looking out, whinnying, and then she stopped. There was a large area full of poop, mostly old poop. Lily reached down with her nose to smell the poop. Earlier, Lily had pooped on top of that same pile of poop that was already there. Marlene spoke, "I think Lily wants me to look at my shit. But there is a lot of shit here. Most of it was here before I came. I'm quick to own my own shit, but I have also been taking responsibility for shit that is not mine."

"I work in a place that dumps on me," Marlene realized out loud. "Do I need to leave Calvary sooner rather than later? Lily, do I need to leave now?" Marlene asked.

Next, Marlene spoke to all of us—the observers and me. "I'm on sabbatical now, and I was planning to wait until I'm back at work in September to tell my boss I want to retire. Maybe I need to tell him now."

With that, Lily walked to Marlene and stopped. Marlene sighed. "I will tell them now, Lily," Marlene said softly. "Yes, I will tell them now."

Lily licked and chewed, as if to say, "Yes, I agree."

Marlene smiled. "Thank you, Lily," she whispered softly as she stroked Lily's neck and began to release some tears. More tears fell as Marlene hugged Lily's neck.

After a few moments, I said to Marlene, "*Now* you can let Lily out of the pen. You'll have to untie the rope to open the gate for her."

Marlene walked forward, and for the first time Lily followed Marlene. Together they walked to the gate. Lily stood patiently while Marlene untied the rope and opened the gate. Lily stepped forward to the edge of the pen. She paused, looking back into the pen at the pile of poop she was leaving behind, and then she turned and faced forward. Lily walked through the gate. With head held high, Lily walked forward, no more looking back. Lily broke into a trot and then a canter. Free and relaxed, Lily disappeared into the misty morning. Marlene wept as she felt her own release and the freedom brought about by her decision to take a stand for her own needs and declare her retirement … Now!

In this later phase of her life, Marlene got to a place where she realized that even with a long life, our time here is short, and that by staying in a job that no longer fulfilled her, she was at risk of losing her vitality to her old patterns. Marlene wanted to spend her later years differently. Lily reflected the intensity and the urgency of Marlene's need to free herself from the years of putting everyone else's needs above her own.

Each of us is unique, and it would be impossible to describe every situation where a person might get stuck. While I may not have described your exact circumstances in these stories, I'm betting you can relate and recognize how it feels to be stuck.

Costs of Staying Stuck

Allowing yourself to stay stuck comes with a cost to your health and your relationships. Feeling stuck can make you tired, drained, apathetic. Maybe you've become numb, and you don't feel anything at all. No zest for life. No inspiration. Nothing to look forward to. Or maybe you are restless, unable to relax or settle. You can't sleep. You may feel detached, like you are living someone else's life, or perhaps it feels like everyone else's needs are more important than yours. Your heart aches for the feeling of freedom to pursue the life you desire. Something in you wants to run away from this life, to run toward your dream, but you don't. Maybe you've recognized this and you have tried to address it, but so far, nothing has worked. Something is in your way. You are stuck, and it sucks!

I understand. I have experienced this kind of stuck, and I know what it feels like. I also know that reading this (or any) book is not going to magically get you unstuck or change your situation because reading a book alone will not fix your problem or bring lasting change to your life. To get unstuck, it's not enough to simply recognize that something is not working for you, and you want it to change. Recognition is a step, but it is not enough to make it happen. You need awareness *and* action. In order to realize a breakthrough, you must first bring awareness to what is keeping you stuck, and then you must take action to change it. While this book can't make the change for you, I do believe that reading it can help you gain a better understanding of yourself. It can move you to a greater awareness of what is keeping you stuck and ways of breaking free.

Before we go on, I feel it is important to note that most people wanting a breakthrough find that they need additional support in the form of a guide, coach, mentor, or facilitator who can be an external observer and offer feedback on the things they cannot see. As motivational speaker Les Brown says, "You can't see the picture when you are in the frame."

I recommend finding someone who can help you bring awareness to what's in your way—what's blocking you from feeling the freedom to make a change and move forward with your life.

Change follows awareness. Awareness is the first step, so let's start there.

2

What's Your Story?

"What's your story?" Growing up, my mom would ask us this question all the time. She didn't ask "How are you doing?" or "What's up?" These questions did not elicit enough information. She wanted to know more. How we were doing and what we were up to were important to her, but these questions might limit the response, and she wanted to know anything and everything we were willing to share. In response to mom's question "What's your story?" we were free to include any details about our self, our day, our situation, anything we felt was important or meaningful.

Everyone likes stories. For entertainment, we love to watch stories on TV, or go to the movies or a play, or read books. Life lessons are often best understood through stories. We learn through story in the form of a fable that helps to illustrate a point. We like to share our own stories, and we like to listen to other people's stories over dinner or around a campfire.

You've probably heard the saying "There are two sides to every story." Each character or real person in a story has their own perspective and interpretation, so the tone and color of a story can change based on who is telling it. Even facts can be perceived differently by people. Without the storyteller's perspective and interpretation, all you have is a list of details.

So . . . what's your story? In your story, you are the main character and the storyteller. You see circumstances and events from your perspective, and you repeat them to yourself as stories. The other characters in your story are the people in your life, and their roles are based on who they are to you and how you relate to them. You'll say the things that happen in your story are good or bad, happy or sad, depending on your interpretation—how you see them, how you feel about them, and what you see possible for the future.

Lynne Twist, global activist and founder of The Soul of Money Institute, says "We don't live in the world. We live in the conversations we have about the world."[1] These conversations are the stories we tell ourselves and others about ourselves and our lives, and they dictate how we feel about who we are and our role in the world. Our stories determine our overall attitude about how life works, how we feel about other people, and whether we perceive their treatment of us as good or bad, fair or unfair. Challenging situations and circumstances can take on a color of hardship or opportunity in our stories, and thus govern how we feel about what is happening and the actions we choose to take, or not. The way we tell stories also indicates whether we feel that life happens "to" us, or whether we take an active role and responsibility for how our life turns out.

One night, in November of 2016, my husband was recharging the battery for a piece of photography equipment. He checked it before we went to bed, and it still needed some time on the charger, so he left it plugged in. Around 10:30 p.m., I awoke to a very loud and unusual sound, so I got up to investigate. As I moved through the house nothing seemed out of the ordinary. When I entered the mud-room, our smoke detector started to beep. Those darn low-battery signals always happen in the middle of the night. As I proceeded to investigate the cause of the unusual sound, I rolled my eyes knowing I'd have to replace the battery before I could go back to bed.

Our mudroom leads to the garage, and I had a sense that's where the sound was coming from. I reached out my hand to open the door to the garage, and as I gripped the handle I noticed its warmth. And then all at once I heard the sound of fire crackling, I smelled smoke, and I realized that the sound that woke me up was the fire roll-up door between the photo studio and the garage slamming shut, AND the smoke detector was beeping because of REAL smoke from a FIRE IN THE GARAGE! I quickly closed the door. "Get up everybody, we have a fire in the garage," I shouted to my husband and kids. "Get your shoes and a jacket, and get outside!"

From that moment, we each had a different experience of what happened. Unbeknownst to me, my brave husband didn't put his shoes on or get his jacket, as I had ordered. He went, barefoot and in his underwear, directly into the garage, grabbed the fire extinguisher, and started to put out the fire. On his way, he called out for someone to dial 911. "I will," said our daughter, Michaella. I continued toward my closet for my shoes and jacket and then grabbed leashes for our dogs and headed outside. "Mom! Dad is in there! He's in the garage . . . in his underwear!" Michaella said to me, frantically, while still on the phone with the 911 dispatcher. I quickly put the dogs in my Suburban with my son, and then I joined my daughter on the front lawn. By then, the fire was out. My husband had opened the garage door and pulled his truck out onto the street. Then we saw him grab his cases of camera equipment from the smoldering cabinets and bring them out to the driveway . . . barefoot and shirtless, but somehow wearing pants.

Just then, the fire engine arrived, and the firefighters began helping him remove the rest of his equipment. Next, they hosed down the smoldering cabinetry and burnt items to make sure the fire did not reignite, and they checked to make sure the attic was clear. It was a strange sight to see all these firefighters in their full safety uniforms while my husband was wearing only his pants.

When the fire captain interviewed us, we each had a slightly different story to tell. We had all participated in the same event, but each of us had a unique experience of what happened. Our stories did not contradict each other, but they were not the same story either. My husband experienced being in the garage with the fire, while Michaella had the experience of worrying about her dad, knowing he was in the garage with the fire, and I didn't know he had gone into the garage until after the fire was out. When we remember the experience of the fire, each of us remembers different emotions and different feelings.

It took months to repair all of the fire damage to the garage and photo studio, and as you can imagine, we've retold this story many times. Parts of the story evolved and took on a new tone as we learned more about what had happened, and as we went through the process of reconstruction.

My husband's story was that he was so proud of how each of us handled the situation. Without any discussion, we each took on a necessary role, and nobody panicked. I made sure the kids and dogs were safe, while he used the fire extinguisher to put out the fire. Michaella made the phone call, and our son sat with the dogs to keep them calm and out of the way of the firefighters.

How about my story . . . was my husband really brave or was he reckless? The next morning, we could see that the fire was only inches away from the gas line to our water heater when he put it out. From my perspective, he saved our house from being destroyed by the fire. Grabbing a fire extinguisher never entered my mind. Not only did he think of a fire extinguisher, he used it, and he saved our house. A few days after the fire, the fire inspector came out to investigate the cause of the fire. He showed us evidence that the air a few inches above my husband's head had reached 800 degrees. He said if my husband had been any taller, he could have singed his lungs and died in our garage. It was a shock to see how close my husband was to losing his life when saving our house. I mean, I knew what he had done was dangerous, but I didn't realize just how dangerous, and neither did he. How I decide to interpret his actions, as brave or reckless, will determine the tone of my story. In my story, he is brave!

The story continues. For my husband, managing the cleanup and reconstruction was a lot of work. Several things were damaged that could not be replaced exactly as they were. He could have been angry and irritated. He could have felt victimized by this event and overwhelmed by the work ahead of him.

Instead, his perspective was to see an opportunity to reassess his workspace and his equipment needs. He decided not everything that was damaged needed to be replaced. Some of his equipment was outdated, and the fire helped him let go of it. He purchased newer equipment that is smaller, lighter, and more efficient. The photo studio had to be repainted, so he had an opportunity to change the colors and the look of it, but instead he decided to restore it to the way it was, making him feel even better about what he had chosen in the first place. His workspace is now back in order, just like it was, but better.

I'm sure my family will be telling the story of the garage fire for years to come. But what I'd like you to see is that the fire is not really the story. The fire was the event. The story is how each of us interpreted this event and how we perceive its impact on our lives. My story is that I have a brave husband, and I trust him to take care of our family. However, if my story had been that my husband was more worried about his photo equipment than being there for our children and me, it would have set our marriage on a completely different and destructive trajectory. This is the power of the stories we tell ourselves. They literally direct the course of our lives.

Whatever is happening in your life, your story is what you tell yourself and other people about it. If you are feeling stuck, then you have a story about why you are stuck and what is keeping you stuck. This story is your interpretation of the circumstances and events connected to and contributing to your feeling of being stuck. This interpretation is based on your perspective, and your perspective comes through a lens created by your beliefs, fears, and habits. It is through this lens that you view and interpret the world, thus creating the story you have about the world.

A lot of times, I'll work with a person who has become aware that they have an old story that is in the way of accomplishing their current aims. They recognize a desire to step into a new story so that they can move forward. But despite their best efforts, they are unable to change or leave the old story behind. Usually, this is because the old story has deep roots. For example, when an interpretation of events is tied to a belief system, before you can unhook from the story, you'll need to address the beliefs.

3

Beliefs

Each person has a unique set of beliefs. Our individual beliefs originate from the belief systems of our ancestral history, family, community, and culture, and they evolve through our life experiences. Beliefs form the foundation of our values and influence our habits, patterns, attitudes, and fears. The lens through which we perceive and interpret the world is colored by our beliefs. An example of this is demonstrated in the saying "looking through rose-colored glasses," which means seeing something as better than it actually is. Our beliefs influence the way we operate in our lives, our expectations of what life will bring, and the story we have about it.

Some beliefs are easily identified, while others are more difficult. They can be conscious or unconscious. Our conscious beliefs are the ones we know about. We are aware of them, and we accept their influence on our lives. Unconscious ones reside in the shadows. We are not aware of them, and we are not aware that they influence us.

When we are born, we inherit an existing system of beliefs, and we are completely dependent on the care of others who live within this belief system. As we grow, we know instinctively that our survival hinges on finding good favor and acceptance from our caregivers, so we begin to track and learn the boundaries of what's acceptable to them and what is not.

Have you seen a small child reach for an object with the intention of picking it up, and as they do, glance at their parent to see if they'll get a look of approval or the disapproving no, don't touch that? This is a child testing the boundaries. At some point in the child's development, the do not touch look will elicit the question "Why not?" as the child seeks to better understand the belief system behind the boundaries.

The belief systems we are born into are multi-layered and complex. The location and culture where we are born and raised form the basic container of our belief system. Within that culture, we are born into a community with an even more specific set of beliefs, including customs, religion, etc. And within that community, we are born into an extended family and an immediate family, where our parents usually form the core of the belief system we inherit.

Civil laws are based on the belief systems of the culture and the community. Our views of what is right and wrong are based heavily on the beliefs of our parents, followed by the civil laws and religious beliefs of our culture and community. Our belief system in action becomes our behaviors.

Acceptable behavior differs from one culture to another. In the United States, many children, some as early as three years old, are asked the question "What do you want to be when you grow up?"

In this culture, it is a generally accepted belief that a person can choose the job or role in society that they wish to pursue. We have a cultural belief in the right to life, liberty, and the pursuit of happiness. But not all cultures share this belief.

In some cultures, a boy is expected to take on the trade or craft of his father. If his father is a blacksmith, then he will be a blacksmith. If his father is a farmer, then he will be a farmer. There is no question, no opportunity to pursue another outcome. Forget about becoming a musician or a painter or a chef.

An individual family's experience can shift their beliefs to differ from their cultural community. For example, even in a culture that allows for a person to choose their own role in life, their own mate, etc., parents who experience financial hardships or low economic status often push their children to pursue careers that the parents deem financially lucrative, or they push their children into an arranged marriage for financial stability, regardless of the individual child's own desires or interests.

Even when it's not so overt, as parents, we often have a picture of what we want for our children. We think we know what is best for them based on our own experience, and we do our best to infuse them with our beliefs. Our parents did the same with us, and their parents did the same with them, and so on and so on. Each of us is indoctrinated with beliefs based on the experiences of previous generations, and many of these beliefs are outdated or no longer relevant. The old story can be formulated out of a cultural or familial belief that doesn't fit who we are now, or even make logical sense. Continuing to live this story keeps us stuck in the past and holds us back from our potential.

Consider the effects of the Great Depression on the belief systems of those who lived through it and the generation that followed. Many incidents of hoarding and collecting clutter have been traced back to a belief in scarcity and the habit of saving everything brought on by the Great Depression. The attitude was that to throw anything away was wasteful and accumulating things was part of the American Dream. Let's look at the beliefs that might come from this:

- Accumulating things is good; it makes you who you are; it is a sign of success.

- If you are a good American, you need to accumulate stuff.

- If you ever throw anything away you are being wasteful, so you should save everything.

- It is better to spend money storing your stuff than to throw anything away.

Now let's look at how these beliefs have shown up in our culture. The self-storage industry reported $22 billion in revenue in 2016. Industry statistics in 2016 also showed that 8.96% of US households rented a self-storage unit, and self-storage companies employed 172,000 people. With 7.3 sq. ft. of self-storage space for every man, woman, and child in the United States in 2016, it was physically possible that every American could stand—all at the same time—under one giant canopy of self-storage roofing.[2] Of course, not everyone using self-storage is doing so because of beliefs that stem from the Great Depression. Many people use self-storage temporarily while remodeling their home, when moving, or if their new home or office isn't ready when they move out of the old one. The reasons people use temporary storage differ from the reasons people use long-term storage. Either way, the belief is the reason behind the action.

Notice what beliefs you may have about whether to store things or throw them away. How do your beliefs influence what you do with your stuff? Whatever you come up with is part of your story. If that story is working for you, if you feel satisfied with how you are storing or not storing stuff, then keep your story and move on. But if it is not working for you, if you feel irritated or uneasy about your story, then maybe you are holding on to an old belief, or maybe you are being influenced by someone else's belief. With this awareness, you can reflect on what is true for you and think about the new story that you'd like to move toward.

A Belief Is Not a Fact

Here's the key: a belief is not a fact, and a belief is not necessarily the truth. Sometimes we get stuck because we are living as if a relative truth is an absolute truth. An absolute truth has to be true for every being, everywhere, at all times—past, present and future, and there are very few absolute truths. Most of what we think of as an absolute truth is really a universal truth. A relative truth is something that is true for me, but it is not necessarily true for others. Let's look at the difference.

The sun rises in the east and sets in the west. Here on Earth, this is a universal truth. It is true for all Earth's inhabitants. Gravity is also a universal truth. Here's another one: Christmas Day is on December 25th. Whether or not you celebrate Christmas, we can agree that all over the world, the date of the Christmas holiday is December 25th. However, if I say, "Christmas comes in the winter," not everyone would agree. This statement is true for those of us living in the Northern Hemisphere, but for my friends living in Australia, or anywhere in the Southern Hemisphere, Christmas comes in the summer. The season in which Christmas occurs is relative to our location on planet Earth. Whether or not we choose to participate in the Christmas holiday depends upon our cultural, familial, and religious beliefs.

None of this is a problem until we mistake our beliefs for the truth. When we live as if our beliefs and opinions are the one and only truth, our story takes on a rigidity that can ostracize or demonize others who have different beliefs and lock us into a life that doesn't fit.

When we are young, the beliefs we inherited may appear to be absolute truth, but as we grow and develop into adulthood, our own life experiences will either challenge or affirm our inherited beliefs. In many cases, we will discover that some of our inherited beliefs are not our own. Through reflection and conscious awareness, we can integrate a new belief or edit an old one. Sounds simple enough. But updating inherited beliefs doesn't always happen easily. When our beliefs are so deeply ingrained that they reside in the unconscious, we may feel a sense of conflict that we are unable to identify, and this can lead to a state of stuckness.

Sometimes we get stuck because we are pretending to agree with someone else's belief out of fear for what might happen if we told our truth.

Our beliefs influence our fears, and both beliefs and fears influence our habits. Our habits can reinforce our beliefs and fears. Since these are interconnected, it can be difficult to talk about one without referencing the others. As we explore beliefs, fears, and habits in more detail, notice how they influence you in your own life.

4

Fears

Fears are educated into us, and can, if we wish, be educated out.
~ Karl A. Menninger

Not all fear is bad. When my son, Achille, was little, he was always trying to touch things that were hot, especially the stove and the barbecue. I think he was attracted to the flame. During Achille's second birthday party, my husband was cooking meat on the barbecue for our guests. Little Achille kept going over to the barbecue and reaching out with his finger as if he were going to touch it. My husband kept telling him "No, it's hot. Don't touch it." But little Achille didn't understand the danger of touching something hot, so he kept trying.

After several times, my husband took a different approach. As Achille moved to touch the barbecue, he looked at my husband expecting to hear no, but instead my husband said, "Go ahead." So, Achille continued forward and touched the barbecue. Of course, he burned his finger and started to cry. My husband promptly brought him inside to get ice for his finger. After that day, Achille never touched the hot barbecue again, and if we told him something was hot, he avoided touching it.

The mechanism of fear is part of our survival instinct. We are born with it. However, most fears are a learned fear of something. A healthy fear of getting burned helps us avoid pain and even death. Fear is beneficial when it alerts us to danger and keeps us safe.

The mechanism of fear and the fear of something are not the same thing. The mechanism of fear is a bodily response. When our brain perceives a threat, certain body systems kick in, releasing chemicals and hormones. Neural activity increases, and bodily responses (like sweating and increased heart rate) occur causing a highly aroused state. It doesn't matter if the stimulus is something environmental or a thought, or whether a threat is real or imaginary, the bodily response is the same. This means we can feel fear even when no real danger is present. The learned fear of something is a concept in our mind where we associate some kind of danger with the object of our fear. If this association is strong enough, our mind will trigger the bodily response of our fear mechanism.

While some fears can keep us safe, not all fears are rational. Let's look at the fear of spiders. Many people dislike spiders to some degree, but seeing a spider does not stop them from carrying on with their day. Some people choose to squish a spider if they find one in their house. Rather than killing them, I prefer to relocate spiders outside. Those with arachnophobia have an irrational fear of spiders, and they may experience an extreme reaction to seeing one. While most spiders won't hurt you, a mild fear response at the sight of a black widow spider is warranted because they are poisonous. However, if the fear of spiders keeps you from getting out your lawn mower because there might be spiders in the shed . . . then it's keeping you stuck . . . and your lawn is likely to become overgrown.

True fear is a survival response to real danger, yet we tend to give in to all sorts of other fears that threaten nothing other than the ego. Most of us do not live in an environment where we are in danger on a daily basis, but many people experience the feeling of fear in their daily lives. Unwarranted fear can hold us back from taking a stand for something we care about or from pursuing a dream.

Most unwarranted fears that keep us stuck are triggered by beliefs and an underlying need for security and acceptance, which are connected to our instinct for survival. For example, it is common for a person to stay in a job they dislike rather than leave to start a business because they fear the loss of a steady income. If you associate your current job with safety and security because it pays your bills, leaving it could be a perceived threat to your survival needs—food, clothing, shelter, etc.—and this fear can keep you stuck in a job you hate, feeling unfulfilled.

There is one fear for all social animals, humans included, that trumps all other fears and is the most common fear that keeps us stuck. There are many versions, but they all have their roots in the same base fear: the fear of being isolated or separated from the group. For a social animal, this is the worst thing that can happen; it means death.

Throughout history, and still in some places today, managing the basic needs of water, food, and shelter takes a lot of effort and most of the day. In nearly all societies, if you ran out of water, the community would join together to find water. But if you were alone with a broken ankle and you ran out of water, you might die of dehydration.

Even today in our modern society, being injured and alone can be a death sentence. The futility of a human being attempting to survive alone in the wilderness is exemplified in *Into the Wild* by Jon Krakauer. This book tells the tale of how a young man, Christopher McCandless, died alone at only twenty-four years of age in the wilderness of Alaska in 1992. Christopher set out on a solo journey into the Alaskan wilderness, and he died four months later due to starvation and complications from eating poisonous seeds. His journal entries indicated he was too weak to forage for food. He was alone; there was no one to help him.

The fear of being isolated or separated from the group manifests itself in many ways such as fear of rejection, fear of abandonment, fear of ostracization, and the more extreme fear of excommunication.

Like beliefs, fears are multi-layered. Many fears present as one thing on the surface while the root fear remains hidden or unconscious. We have to work through the layers to get to the root fear. Let's examine the layers in the fear of pubic speaking.

Surveys have shown that the fear of death ranks very closely with the fear of public speaking. Why? Because our social survival instinct is hardwired into our biology. Those who fear public speaking don't really fear speaking. They speak one-on-one or in small groups all the time. What they fear is the embarrassment of performing badly, backed up by the fear of being perceived as incompetent, which ties to the fears of loss of employment (or loss of clientele), loss of income, loss of home, and loss of the ability to provide for one's survival needs. These fears can contribute to a lowered sense of value or self-esteem, which means loss of identity, which equates to loss of life. As a social animal, our sense of value and our ability to contribute value are the keys to inclusion, and inclusion is essential to survival. This is why we spend so much time worrying about what other people think about us.

In reality, there is no known cause of death resulting from public speaking, and the layers of fear we just explored are not tied to any reality of what is going to happen. If we examine our fears, layer by layer, we can get to the root and realize where our fears are unfounded. Unexamined fears are likely to keep us stuck, preventing us from reaching our potential and realizing our dreams.

Let's look at a few more ways the fear of being isolated or separated from the group can show up. By calling out the different ways this fear manifests, we can help bring awareness to an unconscious fear. The fear of judgment is another form of the fear of rejection and the fear of ostracization. Also related is the fear of failure and the often misnamed, fear of success. Do any of these fears ring a bell? Ding! I've got one ringing for me.

When I was in the seventh grade, I aced all my classes. The small private school I attended had a combined seventh and eighth grade, and they rotated the curriculum every year. My academic skills were well above my grade level, and the school administration gave me the opportunity to skip eighth grade and go right into ninth grade. That meant high school. Of course, I jumped at the opportunity.

While starting high school early was great for me academically, it was socially painful. My old classmates felt like I deserted them because I went into high school, and they were still in junior high. Many of my new classmates were struggling to get passing grades, and they resented that school was easier for me. Schoolmates from both classes called me School Girl and Teacher's Pet. I didn't fit in with either class. I felt alone.

From this experience, I developed what I thought was a fear of success. I was more successful than my classmates, and they became jealous of me. I felt they didn't like me anymore, and I lost my confidence. I started to question who I was. I even sabotaged myself by earning my first and only F on a project, and the only C on my school transcript, all to try to prove that I was just like them . . . so they would like me again.

My fear of success led me to avoid attention or acknowledgment when I did a good job. When someone offered me a compliment, I would respond in a way to deflect it, and this became a habit. I tried to avoid attention for my success, so I could avoid the rejection that came with it.

During my SkyHorseEGE™ certification program in 2010, as part of the training we each lead a round pen session for one of our classmates. It was the second day of this exercise, and there were only a few of us left to participate. I'd had a conversation outside of class with Ashley, so when it was time to volunteer I said I'd lead, and she volunteered to go into the round pen. In that moment, my full focus was on helping Ashley. I asked the right questions to help her progress, and I was quiet in just the right places, allowing the horses to connect and deliver their message. I was moved by what Ashley got from her experience, and I was inspired by the sense of flow that I felt as the facilitator.

When class ended that day, I received a lot of compliments from my classmates. And I became very uncomfortable. Of course, I wanted to do a good job for Ashley's sake, and I wanted Ariana to see I was *getting it* by practicing the principles she taught us. But I didn't want to do *too good* of a job. I didn't want my classmates to become jealous of me and start to dislike me because I could do something they didn't feel they did as well. It was a strange thing . . . to want to do my best, and at the same time to feel so uncomfortable when I succeeded. I have come to realize I did not fear success. What I feared was a repeat of the rejection I experienced in high school.

In fact, the fear of success is a bogus fear. It does not exist. No one fears being successful. It's what we think will happen as a result of our success that we fear. And sometimes, being successful leads to others rejecting us.

The fear of rejection that began during my high school experience followed me into my adult life, as did my habit of deflecting compliments. It didn't matter if the compliment was related to my work or to something I was wearing, I would deflect it. I would look for ways to transfer the compliment to someone else or to belittle what I had done. Until one day when my coach, J Shoop, called me on my habit.

He pointed out to me that deflecting a compliment disrespects the person who is offering it. He helped me change my habit of deflecting compliments to accepting them by simply saying "Thank you."

You can see how the layers of fear showed up for me with the fear of rejection looking like it was a fear of success. Recognizing both layers has been helpful for me in bringing more awareness to when and how my fear shows up, and becoming aware of my habit that was related to my fear gave me a tangible way to make a shift and break the cycle. Remember, our beliefs, fears, and habits are interconnected. Addressing one aspect will affect the others. Let's take a closer look at habits.

5

Habits

Habits are actions, attitudes, and thoughts that occur automatically and repeat when triggered, often without awareness or conscious choice. Habits are like autopilot. They help us do simple and repetitive tasks without having to think too much, saving brainpower for more complicated tasks, learning new skills, and problem solving. Thousands of habits help us run the routines of our daily lives. We have habits for the way we cook dinner, the way we clean house, and the way we fold laundry.

Habits make a lot of things easier. Think about when you learned to drive. At first, each step was a new skill. Putting your foot on the break. Turning the key to start the engine. Checking your mirrors. Putting the car into gear. There was a lot to think about and pay attention to all at once. Do you remember how that was for you? It was a long time ago for me, but while teaching my daughter to drive, I watched her go through this tedious process.

After a while, most of the steps involved in driving become a habit. Unless you are in an unfamiliar vehicle, you don't have to think about what to do to start your car and get on the road. If you drive to a familiar destination, you can even make your turns and lane changes by habit. Unless something out of the ordinary occurs, like road construction or an accident, you can get to your destination with little or no conscious thought about the activity of driving.

Have you ever been driving your car and you realize that for the last mile or two or ten, you were thinking about something completely unrelated to the action of driving? There you were with hands on the wheel, foot on the gas, staying in your lane, and keeping proper distance from the car in front of you all while rehearsing a conversation that you planned to have with your boss or partner. Your subconscious mind was carrying out the habit of driving while freeing up your conscious mind to think about your upcoming conversation. This is the nature of habits. While habits help us get a lot of things done, their subconscious nature can make them difficult to change.

Habits can begin in all sorts of ways, and most habits are formed to avoid pain and discomfort or to experience pleasure. We tend to label habits as good or bad. Most of us would consider brushing our teeth twice a day to be a good habit and smoking cigarettes to be a bad habit. I really enjoy my morning coffee. It's a big deal for me. Each morning when I wake up, I have a habitual thought about my coffee, and I have a habitual attitude that it's worth getting up because I get to have my coffee. I put on my robe and slippers (to avoid the discomfort of the cold floor on my feet), I use the bathroom, and I make a beeline to the Nespresso machine. The pleasure of my coffee habit helps me start my day.

As children, when we learn a new skill we often copy the way our parents or other adults do it, and when we get praise for doing a good job or doing it right, their way becomes our habit. In some cases, we do it their way to avoid the pain of being scolded for doing it wrong. Think about the way you fold your laundry. My mom always folds the towels in a certain way. I learned to do it the same way, and I keep doing it that way because they make a uniform stack on the shelf. Seeing a neat stack of towels gives me a feeling of pleasure. I also have habits that help me avoid pain. Before I take a pot or dish out of the oven, I get out my potholders. By using them, I avoid the pain of getting burned.

My old habit of deflecting compliments was also to avoid pain. It supported my old story that I needed to keep myself and my accomplishments small so I didn't attract too much attention, so no one would be jealous of me . . . in order to avoid the pain of rejection. Only very small successes were okay. This habit, along with the fears and beliefs that made up my *old story*, held me back. Changing my habit to one of accepting compliments and saying thank you has helped me shift to a new story: my success benefits other people, and they appreciate my services and contributions. Now I can accept compliments without the discomfort I used to feel.

A child who grows up in an abusive home will form a habit of reading the moods and expressions of the abusive parent, and develop strategies and responses to avoid the pain of the abuse. Any strategy or response that reduces or prevents the abuse will become a habit. This is a valuable skill for an abused child. But later in life, this person may be in a situation where they need to establish a boundary with, say, a co-worker. If that co-worker's mood or expression triggers a habitual response, then the person may be unsuccessful in setting the boundary. The person may not even be conscious of their habitual response and the obstacle it is creating. While the habit was helpful as a child, it is not serving them in their current situation.

Marlene's experience as a young girl in an abusive home established beliefs and fears that led to a habit of putting everyone else's needs above her own. It was part of her pattern, and it's what all the people in her life expected from her. Marlene also had an unconscious habit of smiling when things were not working. Remember her family credo to put on a good face and present your best? On the outside she was smiling, but on the inside she was unhappy. Her outer expression was not authentic to how she really felt. She didn't mean to be inauthentic, and she didn't even know she was. Smiling to hide her embarrassment or discomfort was a strategy that had served her well as a child, but as an adult, this habit made it difficult for Marlene to acknowledge or express when something was not working for her.

We noticed that when Marlene described a situation that was frustrating her she smiled and nodded yes while she told us about it. When we let her know that her outer expression did not match the experience she was describing, it helped Marlene become aware of when she was smiling, and as a result, she started to check in with herself to see if the smile matched how she was feeling inside. She would pause to connect with her inner feelings and then allow an authentic outer expression to surface. By the end of the week, Marlene's entire face had relaxed, and she stopped smiling when things were not working for her, and when she was truly happy her smile lit up the room.

Try this. Think of something that is upsetting to you. Now try to say what it is out loud while smiling. Do this while looking in the mirror. Smile and start your statement like this "It makes me really upset when . . ." Could you feel how it was forced? How did your body feel as you spoke?

Some of us have a habit of saying things we don't mean in order to protect someone else's feelings or to hide our own feelings. Doing this on a small scale from time to time in an effort to be polite or as a social courtesy is normal, and it's not likely to cause you to feel stuck. However, if you are afraid to say how you really feel about something that is important to you, and you've developed a habit of pretending to not feel a certain way, this inauthentic expression can be what's keeping you stuck.

Your story gives you the clues of where to look. If I asked you "What would happen if you allowed your true feelings to be expressed?" your answer would include a story about what would happen based on what you fear and your underlying contributing belief.

Our habitual expressions and body positions can keep us stuck in unproductive moods and attitudes. For a long time, I had a habit of looking down. I did it when I walked and even when I rode my horse. My riding instructor was always reminding me to look up. I can now see that this habit was connected to my habit of deflecting compliments and my fear of rejection. If I looked down, maybe I could avoid being noticed. It was a way to keep myself small and not assert my energy into a situation. In my role as facilitator and teacher, I was able to see how this habit got in my way, so I worked to change it.

It's not always bad to look down. There are times I need to be careful where I put my feet, so looking down is important. But if my focus is always down I can't be fully present or engaged with my surroundings. Occasionally, I catch myself looking down when I don't need to, and I quickly shift my focus.

Another place our habits can get us stuck is in relationships. Our habits make us predictable to other people, and sometimes we get stuck in relationship patterns where the people in our lives like what we do for them or what we let them do, and they take advantage. For example, maybe you are a generous person, and you have a habit of picking up the check when you go out to eat with friends or family. You appreciate the people in your life and you want to do something nice for them. Then one day, you notice that you are always the one paying for meals, and you wish someone else would pick up the tab once in a while. But everyone is so accustomed to your habit of paying that they have developed a habit of letting you pay. You're stuck footing the bill.

It's no secret that humans seek comfort. We all get comfortable with what is familiar and predictable. Habits are familiar and predictable. Our beliefs and fears are familiar and predictable too. Even if we don't really like what's familiar, we become attached because it is comfortable. And this is why habits get us stuck. We are more likely to stay the same, even if the change is what we truly want, because change is not comfortable. Change brings unfamiliar feelings and unpredictable experiences, which often make us uncomfortable. Sometimes we are stuck because being stuck has become a habit, and we are comfortable being stuck.

How do we get unstuck? Once we've recognized that we are stuck, the first step to getting unstuck is gaining awareness of what is in our way. We do this by examining our story and by looking at the beliefs, fears, and habits that have influenced our perspective and interpretation. Each of us has a unique belief system and a unique set of fears and habits, and there is no one-size-fits-all way to address these.

Getting unstuck requires getting to know yourself better. It requires a willingness to try on new and unfamiliar perspectives and take new actions, and a willingness to tolerate being uncomfortable.

Contrary to popular belief, it is not enough to change your mind to change your reality. In the personal development field, you will find a lot of teachings presented in a cookie-cutter fashion that say "it's all in your mind" and "change your thoughts, change your reality." It just doesn't work that way. Yes, your mind is powerful, but there are other parts of you that need to be aligned for things to start to change, so that you can get unstuck.

PART 2:

Addressing the Issues

6

Humans Aren't Cookies

When it comes to difficulties and challenges, it's human nature to look for the easiest way out. We want a silver bullet that will solve the problem, and if we can't find one, logic suggests we find a way to simplify it. We look for ways to break a problem down into smaller components. We quantify and qualify those components and study them in detail. We put them into categories, and we create formulas and systems to help us manage the categories.

In Western culture, we like using formulas and systems. They often save time and money, make our lives more efficient, and enable us to do more things. They also help us get predictable, repeatable results—like using a cookie cutter on cookie dough. This approach works well in so many areas of life, such as manufacturing, engineering, agriculture, etc., that we've tried to apply the same principles when working with people. But with people, formulas and cookie-cutter systems only work some of the time, with some of the people. No singular system or solution works for everyone all of the time. Why not? Because . . . humans aren't cookies!

Typecasting by Learning Styles

We've tried a cookie-cutter approach in several ways of working with people. Education is a big one. In the United States, our public school system is designed to educate students in a standardized method, with primarily teacher-centered instruction where activity in the classroom is centered around the teacher, and the focus of the lesson is on distributing facts to students. Students are divided into separate classes by age and sometimes ability, and all students are taught the same material in the same way. While this approach works for a majority of students, many students struggle. Improving student success is a major focus of educators, and they try to identify the issues that inhibit learning and cause some students to struggle.

It has been postulated that a student's learning style is a major factor influencing student success. Beginning in the early 1900s, many theorists studied learning styles. They began creating ways to measure and understand the differences in how students learned. This involved labeling students according to certain criteria and arranging them in categories. Toward the end of the 20th century, psychologists and educators theorized that if they could determine a student's learning style, they could shift teaching styles to match learning styles and improve student success.

In the 1980s, the National Association of Secondary School Principals formed a task force to study learning styles, and learning style models and assessments grew in measure and influence. But further research found matching teaching style to students' learning styles to be expensive and inefficient. In 2009, the Association for Psychological Science (APS) published a report on the scientific validity of learning styles practices, stating that the majority of studies done on learning styles were not properly designed and executed to produce scientifically valid data. Of the few that were done with the appropriate research design, all but one produced negative findings. They concluded that "at present, there is no adequate evidence base to justify incorporating learning styles assessments into general educational practice."[3]

While the article incited critical comments from some defenders of learning styles, David Kolb, who had developed one of the styles that was studied, was quoted in response saying, "The paper correctly mentions the practical and ethical problems of sorting people into groups and labeling them."[4]

"After the 2009 APS report, articles began to appear claiming that learning styles have been 'debunked' and are a 'myth.'"[5] But learning styles are not a myth. People absolutely do have different styles of learning. The myth is that a cookie-cutter type solution creates optimal learning outcomes on a mass scale. This is the myth that was debunked. Educators are not going to find the one "right" approach for all students and all subjects, because it doesn't exist.

Dr. Richard Felter, widely known for his work in engineering education and a teaching and learning scholar, said, "The point is not to match teaching style to learning styles but rather to achieve balance, making sure that each style preference is addressed to a reasonable extent during instruction. The ideal balance among learning style categories depends on subject, level, the learning objectives of the course, and the backgrounds and skills of students."[6]

Many educational institutions have chosen to act as if learning styles are a myth, and remain in their systems of uniformity, utilizing the same teaching methods for all types of learners because it's more convenient and less expensive to keep the existing cookie-cutter approach.[7] But educators owe it to students to acknowledge learning styles and incorporate the knowledge gained, not pretend all students are the same and learning styles don't exist.

Yes, there is a responsibility on the part of the student to take an active role in learning, and there is also a responsibility on the part of the educators to serve their students. In some cases, educators may need to adjust teaching methods based on specific subject matter and learning objectives, and to better serve a variety of students, educators may need to introduce materials and concepts using a variety of teaching methods simultaneously.

Personality Typing

Closely linked to the mapping out of learning styles is the practice of sorting people by personality types. Some learning style models even include personality types in their theory. The study of personality types is ancient. From Hippocrates and his Four Temperaments to the more recent Myers-Briggs Type Indicator (MBTI), philosophers, physicians, and psychologists have sought to solve human problems by sorting people into categories based on the idea that if we fit someone into a category with a pre-set list of characteristics and tendencies, it will narrow down the potential causes of their problems, and outcomes will be better and more predictable.

Personality typing has been widely embraced by the personal development and self-help industry. While this approach has its merits, as with learning styles and education, there is a tendency toward oversimplification. Our human tendency to want the easiest, quickest, and simplest method or outcome has resulted in a market flooded with programs that offer sweeping solutions with a quick fix promise.

We all want problem solving to be easier, and I fully support looking for an easier way, but not at any cost. The two key areas where oversimplification causes trouble are the rigid assessments with narrow and restrictive categories that put people in silos and one-size-fits-all formulaic solutions that can't possibly work for everyone.

Let's explore some categories to see how this works. The categories of Hippocrates' Four Temperaments are sanguine, phlegmatic, choleric, and melancholic, with dual combinations of these (for example, sanguine-choleric or choleric-melancholic). With Myers-Briggs there are sixteen personality type categories determined by four indicators: Extraversion vs. Introversion, Sensing vs. Intuition, Thinking vs. Feeling, and Judging vs. Perceiving. In the learning style models, we see categories like visual learner, aural learner, verbal learner, and kinesthetic learner. The Kolbe Four Action Modes has categories for how people solve problems: Fact Finder, Follow Thru, Quick Start, and Implementor. And the list of categorizing systems and names goes on and on.

The mechanisms for putting people into categories are assessments. To determine the appropriate category, subjects are usually given a questionnaire or test that's tied to some sort of algorithm which scores the test. Assessments are specifically designed to qualify and quantify tendencies, aptitudes, preferences, abilities, etc., and based on the results, filter the subject into the specified categories. Besides fully automated tests, some assessments can be self-administered and self-interpreted, while others are administered and interpreted by an individual trained/certified to do so. Once the category type is determined, there is usually an interpretation or summary that describes the subject in ways that differentiate them from the other category types.

In some cases, the results help us see ourselves the way other people see us, or they help us better understand a loved one or co-worker. If we know that a person is categorized as an introvert, it tempers our expectations of them in group situations, and contributes to our ability to predict their actions and needs. A student with an aural learning style may benefit from listening to a book on tape more than reading the text. If you know your daughter has a sanguine tempera-ment and your son is a Fact Finder, you're not surprised that she sometimes gets in trouble for talking too much in class, and he wants to ask twenty questions about the new rules for course selection at school. As a whole, our human patterns repeat and do present a certain predictability which makes some assessments accurate for a wide range of people, and yet, no singular system of categorization will be a fit for everyone.

Problems arise when an assessment system or interpretation is too rigid. In a rigid assessment system, you will find the questions are designed with a limited selection of responses, which guide the subject into a category through a preset formula; it's like leading the witness in a legal deposition. As they attempt to find one right answer, subjects are sometimes forced to select the closest answer, and they end up being relegated into a category type that doesn't fit.

If the rigidity is in the interpretation, it becomes a trap. It feels good to be seen and understood, so we want to see ourselves in the summary. We want to feel like someone out there gets who we are, so we take the assessment results as fact and we think "This is who I am."

The risk is that we put ourselves into silos, fixed and defined by our category type, with no opportunity for change or growth, and we can become stuck in a limiting interpretation of ourselves.

To be clear, I am not against assessment systems. A good assessment can help to reveal unconscious aspects of who we are and help us understand ourselves better. I have found a variety of assessment systems very helpful, and I use many of them in my work. I am always open to exploring new assessments that might offer additional perspectives or new distinctions. But we are unique in more ways than a personality test or assessment can reveal.

The key distinction here is that I use assessments as a guide, not a rule. Assessments are best used when their role is to reveal clues, not when used as the only explanation or to prescribe the solution. In fact, I'm leery of anyone offering canned solutions for personal growth. This includes any solution that is promised in "five easy steps" or packaged in the wrapping of "just do what I did, and you can get my results."

People's problems are complex. Each person comes into this world with a unique combination of strengths and weaknesses, tendencies, attributes, natural talents and interests, and personality traits, all of which are tempered by our families, environments, and experiences. These aspects of who we are, in combination with cultural and familial influences, give each of us a unique way of seeing and interpreting the world and a unique way of integrating our experiences into our being. A formulaic strategy cannot possibly account for all of the influencing factors. When cookie-cutter solutions don't work, and most of the time they don't, the cost is that the person thinks there is something wrong with them because they didn't get the desired result. They blame themselves and feel even more stuck.

Individual uniqueness makes up the beauty and diversity that is humanity. We have different ways of relating with the environment, and we respond to stimuli in our own unique way. An experience that causes anger in one person may trigger insecurity or compassion in someone else. Some people are more attuned to tactile stimulation, and they tend to relate better with their environment through touch, while others relate better visually. Some people prefer to go to a quiet place of solitude to reflect and process a difficult experience, while other people prefer the company of a trusted friend with whom they can process their experience through conversation.

Even in situations where environmental and external factors are very similar, a person's unique internal constitution will differentiate their responses from others. Consider the differences in siblings. In most cases, siblings are born into the same family, culture, and the same community. My mom is one of eight children. The family includes five girls and three boys, all raised by the same parents, and they shared in many of the same events and circumstances while growing up. Every couple of years, we have a family gathering that brings all eight siblings together, and observing them is fascinating. Physically the family resemblance is unmistakable as they share many outward similarities, but what stands out the most are the things that make them different. For example, my mom is more of an introvert, and she hates making phone calls, while my aunt is outgoing and will pick up the phone to make a call without hesitation. Motherhood has taught me to recognize and respond to uniqueness. My children are not motivated by the same things, they are not always interested in the same things, and they do not respond to situations in the same way. I've learned that I need to parent each one differently.

For example, in trying to teach our children certain life skills and appropriate behaviors, one form of punishment my husband and I have used is to ground them. To be grounded means they have to stay in their rooms, or at least they have to stay at home. They are not allowed to have friends over or go out with friends.

For Kali, my eldest, punishing her by grounding her to her room wasn't much of a punishment, and it certainly did not work as a deterrent for undesired behavior. Kali has always been an avid reader, and she loves being left alone in her room to read. We could take away all sorts of other privileges as part of her punishment, and it was never that bad for her. But for Michaella, my middle child, grounding is a tough punishment and a great deterrent. Michaella is a social butterfly, and it is painful for her to have her social privileges suspended. For my son, Achille, grounding means restriction from video games. For him, this is a formidable punishment and works well as a deterrent.

Whether it's parenting, teaching, leading, or coaching, no one tool, system, process, or formula will work for all people and all situations. Part of the reason people stay stuck is that they try using a one-size-fits-all approach to address their issue, and it doesn't work. This leads to frustration and they give up. Those cookie-cutter methods make it seem so simple, yet they are deceiving because they do work for a few people, just not everybody.

To be truly effective, tools and methods must be fluid and flexible enough to accommodate the wide range of our uniqueness. When searching for personal development support, I recommend looking for a practitioner with a variety of tools in their toolbox who uses an integrated approach that attends to a person as a whole being: mind, body, spirit, and soul.

7

The Mind — It's *Not* All in Your Head

When you reach the point of feeling stuck, it's usually after you've spent an inordinate amount of time going around and around the same issue in your mind without making any progress. When I have this experience, it feels like a little hamster running on a wheel in my head. The wheel spins around and around. As hard as the hamster works, he just keeps going around on the wheel. Busy hamster. Busy mind. When your mind is busy going around and around, around and around, it becomes part of the problem, not the solution.

When we are stuck, we are not likely to find a solution by focusing solely on the mind. The mind is only one aspect of our being, and we perpetuate our stuckness when we put too much emphasis on what it thinks without paying attention to the other aspects of ourselves— our body, spirit, and soul. Still, we do need to include the mind in our process because the mind enables us to gain and retain awareness. Awareness enables us to choose consciously. In order to make any constructive change, we must develop or expand our awareness, and we need our mind working with us, not against us, to do so.

I am fascinated by how the mind and the brain work. I am also fascinated by the differing schools of thought related to the distinctions between the mind and the brain, and how the various perspectives influence the study of the mind. Dualism is a school of thought popularized by René Descartes. While there are varying theories within dualism, dualistic views hold that mental phenomena are in some respects non-physical—that humans have both a mind (non-physical) and a body/brain (physical) that are distinct and separable. The concept of dualism has been demonstrated in movies like *The Shaggy Dog* where the consciousness of a man is transferred into a dog's body, and *Freaky Friday* where a mother and daughter swap minds—the mother's mind transfers into the daughter's body and the daughter's mind into the mother's body.[8]

In contrast, theories of monism do not accept any fundamental division between the mind and body/brain. According to the monistic theory of idealism, consciousness exists before and is the precondition of material existence. Consciousness creates and determines the material and not vice versa. Idealism believes consciousness and mind to be the origins of the material world and aims to explain the existing world according to these principles.

The monistic theory of physicalism conversely asserts that everything is physical, that there is nothing over and above the physical. Closely related materialism is the belief that consciousness (the mind) is a function of the brain, and the mind and consciousness are by-products of material processes, i.e., the biochemistry of the human brain and nervous system, reducing human beings to no more than physiological organisms. I don't know about you, but I am unable to entertain the theories of physicalism and materialism as they lack room for the existence of spirit and soul. My life experiences have revealed the spirit and soul as not only real, but integral to our existence as human beings.

These differing theories of the mind influence the way the mind is studied. In Western culture, the most widely utilized tools for working with the mind, including learning style and personality type assessments, come from the field of psychology. Throughout history, the field of psychology has contributed heavily to personal development and education. I've appreciated the contributions, but in a lot of the work, I've felt something was missing. As I studied its history, I began to see that much of the psychology practiced today is not what it used to be. Within our modern-day definition of psychology—the science of the mind and behavior—I find undertones of physicalism and materialism, which relegate the study of the psyche to the purely physical and measurable.

When the ancient Greeks explored why people do the things they do, psyche, the root word of psychology, had a different meaning than it does in today's Western culture. The word psyche is from the Greek word *psykhe* meaning soul, mind, spirit, life-breath, one's life, the essence of a person (or place or thing, figuratively), usually thought to consist of one's thoughts and personality. Greek philosophers Thales of Miletus, Plato, Aristotle, and physician Hippocrates addressed the mind to solve human problems using this more comprehensive definition which persisted through the 17th century. In 1694, we find the first recorded use of psychology in the English language by Steven Blankaart in *The Physical Dictionary*, which refers to "Anatomy, which treats the Body, and Psychology, which treats the Soul."[9]

The modern version of psychology that most of us know today wasn't formed until the late 1800s. It was during this time that Wilhelm Wundt, a German physician, physiologist, philosopher, and professor, was the first person to call himself a psychologist, and he defined psychology as a science apart from philosophy and biology.[10] In 1879, Wundt opened the first formal laboratory for psychological research at Leipzig University. And in 1890, William James, an American philosopher and physician, defined psychology as the science of mental life, both of its phenomena and their conditions. James was the first educator to offer a psychology course in the United States.[11]

As technology advanced, more and more psychologists began to confine their discourse to aspects of the mind that were observable and measurable, and the scientific discipline of psychology became entirely focused on the mind and behavior, leaving out the aspects of the soul and spirit.

Many great findings and beneficial knowledge have come from psychological studies and research. I have friends in the psychology field who are therapists and counselors, and I appreciate the work they do to help people navigate their struggles and move toward a better life. I am grateful for the work that many have done and continue to do to help us better understand the workings of the mind and how they relate to brain function and chemistry in the brain and body. At the same time, I can't help but be saddened by the exclusion of the spirit and soul that prevails in psychology as a science.

With this disconnect, it has become easier for the science of the mind to zero in on the form and function in the brain and put a primary focus on mental processes and the physiological functions associated with the nervous system. These are valid areas of study, but something has gone wrong in the medical field when it comes to treating the mind and the brain. The mind has become segregated from the other aspects of a person, and more and more, the science of psychology views thoughts and emotions solely from a chemical standpoint, reducing joy, sorrow, excitement, and even desire, to hormones, neurotransmitters, and synapses that, more and more, are treated with chemicals over talk therapy or counseling.

As this way of treating the mind has become more pervasive, there's been a sharp rise in the prescribing and use of pharmaceuticals to treat problems of the mind by addressing the physical aspect of the brain's chemistry. For example, the number of Americans using anti-depressants rose by 65% between 1999 and 2014. By 2014, one in eight Americans over the age of twelve reported recent antidepressant use.[12]

It's true, some disorders and mental health issues are chemical in cause and nature, so drug therapy is appropriate. But for many people, pharmaceuticals only mask the symptoms of a core issue. They don't address the underlying cause. Many people with perceived physical problems or those struggling with depression or anxiety are really suffering from a crisis of the spirit or soul.

In 2006, I'd been having a lot of pain in my low back and neck, frequently accompanied by headaches. At one point, I could barely bring my left arm over my head to change my shirt, and every time I got in my car to drive, I had a numb feeling that went all the way down my left leg. Chiropractic care wasn't helping, so I went to an orthopaedic doctor, and he prescribed physical therapy. Some of my symptoms were resolved after a few months of physical therapy, but the core low back pain, neck pain, and headaches persisted. In early 2007, I went to see Dr. Millard, a physiatrist specializing in physical medicine and rehabilitation. Over the course of that year, I did more physical therapy, and Dr. Millard prescribed and treated me with epidural cortisone injections three different times, once in my low back and twice in my neck. The treatments helped with my neck, shoulder, and low back pain, but the headaches not only persisted, they increased.

At one point, I realized I'd had a migraine type headache every day for a whole year. It wasn't always full blown with auras, but the headache never stopped. Day after day, it persisted. I have a high pain tolerance, but the constant, nagging pain started to wear on me. Simple things like doing laundry or going to the grocery store would seem overwhelming on some days. Since the cortisone treatments had not improved the headache, Dr. Millard referred me to a neurologist.

In December of 2007, I went to see Dr. Fung. First, Dr. Fung ordered an MRI to see if I had a brain tumor. Thankfully, the brain scan showed no abnormalities. Dr. Fung then began prescribing medications to try, which I reluctantly took. Each time I visited him, I left with a sample of a new medication to interrupt a migraine. I tried several, and they all gave me side effects worse than the headache itself. The first preventive medication I tried was an anti-seizure medication called Topamax. It made my fingers and toes numb. I felt like I was not quite in my body, and I still had a daily headache.

At my next appointment, as I waited in Dr. Fung's office, I noticed the certificates on his wall. One of them indicated he was on the board or head of the board of certified medical acupuncture. He was not just an acupuncturist, he was a doctor of acupuncture. I much prefer natural medicine, and I was only trying prescription drugs as a last resort. I got excited that maybe as a neurologist and acupuncturist, Dr. Fung could help me without the drugs.

When Dr. Fung came in to see me, I asked about the possibility of his acupuncture treatment, but my hopes were quickly dashed by his response.

He told me he only used acupuncture as a last resort.

When I asked why, he said that he can see four patients in an hour treating them with medication, but with acupuncture, he can only treat one patient per hour, and we hadn't tried enough medications for him to consider me for acupuncture.

I was desperate to feel better, and without any other apparent choice, I left his office with my next preventive prescription, a cocktail of naproxen sodium and a low dose of Nortriptyline, which is an antidepressant.

After a couple of weeks on the new drug combo, I had my first day with no headache. Finally, some relief! But not without side effects.

I was feeling better for several months, until the naproxen sodium irritated my stomach, and I had to stop taking it. The Nortriptyline was not as effective alone, but the headache frequency and intensity were less than before, so I kept taking it.

While on the Nortriptyline, I noticed that it was harder and harder to wake up in the morning. My mind wasn't as sharp as it used to be. I felt a low grade but continuous sense of detachment from my life and from myself. I didn't get excited about things the way I used to. I didn't feel invested in or connected to what I was doing. My emotions were dulled. It was like I was observing my life happening, rather than living and feeling it. This was not how I wanted to live. Continuing in this way was unacceptable to me, and I wanted to get off the medication, but I didn't want to go back to having a headache all the time. I felt stuck.

I didn't know it at the time, but I was having a crisis of the soul. There was something I was missing in my life that I needed to address. The physical pain issues combined with the year of headaches were a plea from my psyche, through my body, to pay attention. Taking advantage of the anti-inflammatory effect of the cortisone to break the pain cycle in my body made sense. But addressing the headache with medication only treated symptoms and prolonged the process of identifying my true problem. I spent two years, between the spring of 2008 and 2010, on Nortriptyline before understanding the true issue and finding my way off the meds.

I had been out of the workforce since 2000 when I went on maternity leave to have my second child. While on maternity leave, I began doing the books for my husband's photography business, and it worked out so well, I never went back to my corporate job. Then in May 2003 my son was born, and three months later, we sold our house and bought a major fixer-upper. For the next two years, all my time was devoted to taking care of three small children, managing a major house remodel, and keeping the books for my husband's business. I'd always wanted to be a stay-at-home mom, and during that time, with everything I was doing, it felt fulfilling.

But once the remodel was complete and my children were all in school, I had more time to myself, and I started to feel insecure about not working. I began to question my value, and I started comparing myself to other people. I compared myself to my friends who worked. Most of them had full time jobs, in addition to having families to take care of. They seemed jealous of me and would tell me how lucky I was. It made me feel guilty that I didn't *have* to work outside of the home and that life seemed easier for me than it was for other people. I remember having these thoughts, but at the time, I wasn't conscious of their impact on me, and I did not connect them to my physical pain and headache.

As the pain persisted, and the mundane tasks of my days became more and more difficult, my physical affliction began to drown out my sense of guilt and insecurity. Rather than my friends being jealous of me for not working, they felt sorry for me due to the difficulties I was having. For a while, the headache pain became a screen, buffering me from the judgment of others and my own self-judgment.

After months of being restricted by the headache pain, getting back to health became my main focus because I wanted to be able to take care of my family without feeling overwhelmed. The physical therapy and cortisone injections followed by the headache medications worked to an extent. As the physical symptoms subsided, I recognized a contrast that brought things into a new perspective. When the pain was there, I only noticed the pain, but when it was gone or minimized, I noticed that I didn't go back to feeling the way I'd felt before it started. I didn't have the same feeling of aliveness or sense of purpose and satisfaction with who I was. This contrast gave me a clue as to what was really going on. While being a wife and mother was fulfilling in many ways, I felt like I had more to offer that I wasn't sharing and a purpose that extended beyond just my family. But I didn't know what to do with the awareness or how to go about getting off the meds.

In early 2010, I was invited to a mastermind class to explore Bob Proctor's book *You Were Born Rich*. We had weekly conference calls that were led by Coach J Shoop. After the mastermind class, I enrolled in personal coaching with Coach Shoop. The first course was about setting goals. Coach Shoop helped me realize that while I was helping my husband and children achieve their goals and the shared goals of our family, I did not have any personal goals that were mine. Perhaps because I was not working and bringing home a paycheck, I had not given myself permission to want anything... except my horse. That was my "one thing," and anything beyond that I feared would seem greedy.

I made a list of goals. My list included home improvement and organization projects, a scuba diving vacation, cross country jumping with my horse, improving my relationships with my husband and children, just to name a few. With Coach Shoop's help, I began to explore my gifts, talents, values, and beliefs. I began to recognize the thoughts that moved me in the direction of my goals and the thoughts that were in my way.

With my new tools and practices, I felt I could manage the headaches without medication. In April of 2010, I slowly lowered my dose of Nortriptyline and eventually stopped taking it altogether. A few months later, I had my first introduction to SkyHorse Equine Guided Education™. With Coach Shoop's encouragement, I added it to my list of goals, and initiated one of the most significant life changing experiences of my life.

The drugs did help to break the pain cycle, and I'm grateful for that, but it was not the drugs that got me unstuck. The drugs couldn't address the underlying problem. The physical symptoms were communicating a crisis of the soul, and no drug was going to fix that.

I'm not saying it's bad to use pharmaceuticals. They are necessary for some conditions. But they are not my preference, and I don't believe they were the only way, or the best way, for me to relieve the headaches. The coaching I received and the tools I learned from it were the catalysts I needed to help me get unstuck.

As in my case, it seems all too common in the medical industry for physicians to prescribe pharmaceutical drugs, with all of their side effects, without first trying other non-chemical treatments. A 2012 American Psychological Association article by Brendan L. Smith discusses inappropriate prescribing of medications. He cites the increase in primary care physicians prescribing antidepressants to their patients without any psychiatric evaluation or attempt at psychotherapy as concerning, because many patients may be taking drugs that are inappropriate for their condition. He also cites inappropriate prescribing of anti-psychotic drugs and the medications used to treat ADHD.

Smith's article includes a reference to a study by Hollon, from the Archives of General Psychiatry, 2005, which found psychotherapy to be just as effective as antidepressants in many cases, without the risk of side effects and with lower instances of relapse. The study also found enduring effects from the cognitive therapy that may help prevent the recurrence of depression. Smith goes on to point out that with lower clinician reimbursement rates for psychotherapy and higher out-of-pocket costs to patients, the use of psychotherapy has declined.[13]

I see three primary reasons for the decline in the use of psychotherapy and the increase in prescribing medication. Reason one is money, and reason two is time. Physicians can make more money in less time by treating patients with drugs, and patients can get a cheaper, quicker "fix" by taking drugs. Reason three is that traditional psychotherapy often does not work, and people don't know what else to try. While finding an alternative to psychotherapy can be difficult, drug prescriptions are easy to obtain.

Psychotherapy is what most people think of when they are stuck and seek professional help for life's problems. In this process, loosely referred to as "talk therapy," the therapist and patient sit in chairs having a back and forth dialogue. If you have an issue specific to the mind, psychotherapy may help you find an insight or solution to resolve your issue. Psychotherapy provides a process for looking back at your past and your history to uncover influences and experiences that may have created triggers, or resulted in an unresolved traumatic reaction, or in extreme cases, Post-traumatic stress disorder (PTSD). It can work well if you find a therapist with whom you can develop trust, and if the therapist is able to offer meaningful and productive suggestions that you can implement.

I know many people who have experienced benefits from psychotherapy. I've also worked with many clients who tried psychotherapy and found it didn't work for them. As in many professions, earning an academic degree in psychotherapy and passing the licensing test don't automatically make a person a good therapist.

Attempts at therapy can fail if the individual has a difficult time developing the level of trust with the therapist necessary for this form of treatment to be effective. And unless the patient takes the insights gained and moves toward creating proactive solutions in their life, the sitting in chairs and talking become another version of the hamster wheel. Talking with someone who is an active listener makes us feel heard; the patient might temporarily feel better when they are able to share their story with the therapist, and they might schedule session after session to feel better again, but if no new actions are initiated in the patient's life to bring about a meaningful change, the person will continue to stay stuck.

Sometimes understanding the ways of the mind is not enough to get a new result. Sometimes the barrier to change is not to be found in the mind, so it cannot be resolved there. A tire gauge is the perfect tool for measuring the air pressure in your tires, but it won't help you check your oil or change a spark plug.

I continue to look to psychology for tools and help when it comes to working with the mind and awareness. It was encouraging to find a 2016 article from *Quartz* in which Olivia Goldhill reported on a meeting held by Dan Siegel, professor of psychiatry at UCLA, with a group of forty scientists including psychologists, neurologists, physicists, sociologists, and anthropologists who agreed that the mind extends beyond our physical brain and neurological activity.[14] Their view, which more closely resembles that of the ancient Greeks, recognizes that our mind is not merely an organ that perceives our experience, but an element of the experience itself.

While there's more hope for better tools from psychology, we are multifaceted as individuals and working solely with the mind cannot suffice. We must bring along our tools for understanding the mind as we look at additional tools for addressing our body, spirit, and soul.

8

The Body — Let Me Hear Your Body Talk

Before heading up to the barn to do some work with my horse, Cari, I had a difficult phone conversation with my husband, and I was feeling down and a little overwhelmed. As I walked into the barn, my friends, Barb and Katie, were chatting it up. They paused to say "good morning" to me, and then returned to their conversation. I softly greeted Cari and then moved into her stall with my brush and hoof pick. As I brushed Cari's coat, I couldn't help hearing what Barb was saying to Katie. I wasn't clear on the timeframe of the story, but it clearly took place around a funeral. As I listened, I gathered that it was Barb's husband's sister who had passed away. Barb is a good friend, and I wanted to express my condolences, so I looked for an appropriate break in the conversation to say how sorry I was to hear of her passing.

"Oh, thanks," Barb said. "She was sick for a long time. It's okay." There was some family drama surrounding the funeral, which is what she had been telling Katie about, so she got me up to speed too. As I turned to go back to brushing Cari, Barb seemed like she was getting ready to leave. But then she looked at me and stopped.

"How are you?" she asked. "I mean, are you okay? You don't seem like . . ."

Barb didn't finish her sentence. She could see my eyes filling up with tears, and she knew I wasn't okay. I shared with her how my husband was away on a two-and-a-half-week business trip, and a week after he left, Michaella let her friend drive our car, and they got into an accident. There were no injuries, but the car was totaled. It was a complicated situation and with my husband away, there was an added layer of parenting negotiations and mediation required. I told her I was feeling overwhelmed. I knew it would all be fine, but my emotions were on edge. Once I spilled my beans, I started to feel better. I thanked Barb for listening, and she encouraged me to enjoy my horse as she left the barn.

How did Barb know something was wrong after our initial conversation? It wasn't what I said. In fact, I had tried to engage with her about her husband's sister without giving away the fact that I was feeling down. Whether Barb knew it or not, she was listening to my body talk. She could tell by the way I held by body, my facial expression, and other cues that something wasn't right with me.

We tend to think of communication as the words we say, but science has shown that our attitudes or feelings are constantly being conveyed, and if there's a discrepancy between our words and our body talk, the body talk carries more weight.[15] Each of our bodies continuously broadcasts information about how we are feeling and our prevalent attitudes. All day long, we send and receive communication signals through body language and facial expressions, and most of the time, we don't even realize we are doing it.

Science also shows that the body is able to process more information than the conscious mind. According to scientific research, the human body sends eleven million bits of information per second to the brain, but the processing capacity of the conscious mind is only 50 bits per second.[16] A quick calculation (50 divided by 11 million), and we see that the conscious mind is processing .000005%, or less, of the information available. This means there is a lot more going on around us and in our bodies than our conscious minds are able to pay attention to.

The body is constantly communicating to the brain, sending signals when we are hungry, when we need to use the restroom, when we feel hot or cold, when we feel sad or afraid.

From a biological standpoint, the body is the *first responder,* and the mind comes along after the fact to make up its interpretation.[17] Something changes in the environment, and at eleven million bits per second, information taken in by the body is sent to the brain. After processing a tiny fraction of that information, the conscious mind interprets it. Whatever conclusion the mind makes up about what it thinks happened is founded solely on this limited interpretation, and it's not necessarily the "truth." Sometimes we make a helpful interpretation, and sometimes our interpretations contribute to keeping us stuck.

Our bodies let us know when we are feeling safe and when we are uncomfortable. But we don't always listen. Often, we don't eat when we should, or we keep eating after we're already full. Sometimes we ignore our body's request for movement because we are trying to meet a writing deadline.

The signals and information from our bodies can include input from our five senses, as well as our intuitive senses, biological signals, feelings, and emotions. Some signals, including "gut feelings," come from the literal gut, where the enteric nervous system resides. With its own neural network, the gut has been called a "second brain," and it does a lot more than handle digestion or inflict the occasional nervous pang of "butterflies." This gut intelligence, working in conjunction with the brain, partially controls our mental state and is a key influencer in certain diseases. Signals are also sent from the "heart-brain," a common name used by neurocardiologists to refer to the heart's intrinsic cardiac nervous system. With its intricate network of complex ganglia, neurotransmitters, proteins, and support cells, the same as those of the brain in the head, it is sufficiently extensive as to be characterized as a brain on the heart. In fact, there are more pathways transmitting information from both the heart and the gut to the brain than vice versa.[18]

Most of us ignore or dismiss these signals and information to some degree because our sensitivity and responsiveness get conditioned out of us. Often this occurs as a result of cultural conditioning that we receive from our parents, extended families, and society at large. I've found five ways that this tends to manifest:

1) Suppressing the body's natural expression

2) Learning to ignore or put off our own needs to meet others' needs

3) Protecting others from our feelings

4) Dissociative response to trauma

5) Desensitization due to overstimulation

Suppressing the Body's Natural Expression

Often, parents teach their children to suppress their body's natural expression. It's not socially acceptable to hang out in a store or restaurant with a fussing and crying child. If the episode is brief, most people don't mind, but if it goes on for too long, it becomes disturbing and irritating. Often the child is uncomfortable because they are tired, hungry, or need a diaper change. They've reached the end of their tolerance so they begin to fuss. When the timing is inconvenient for addressing the child's needs, most parents will do whatever they can to hush the child while they finish their shopping or meal. I've certainly had this experience with my own children. I've felt the social awkwardness of a crying child causing a disturbance, and I've been guilty of hushing my children and asking them to ignore their bodily signals while I tried to finish my task.

Learning to control your behavior in public so as not be annoying is one thing, but this teaching extends much farther as the child ages. Males, young and old, are raised with the cultural belief that "boys shouldn't cry," causing them to suppress their feelings and emotions. In addition, females often suppress their emotions due to the societal belief that "girls are too emotional" which can create the impression that females should disregard their own feelings as frivolous, or try to hold them in.

Putting Off Our Own Needs

Putting off our own needs to accommodate the needs of others is a normalized social expectation for most of us, especially females. I learned to be aware of socially appropriate timing and curtail my own needs when I was a little girl. I remember visiting my dad and riding with him in his truck when he was making deliveries to his clients. He had a schedule he was trying to keep, and if I was hungry before he was ready to stop, or if I had to go to the bathroom at an inconvenient time, it would be frustrating to him. I didn't want to upset him, so I did my best to tolerate any discomfort and wait for more convenient opportunities for food and potty breaks. It's important to be socially responsible for the way we respond to our own needs and feelings, but if we go too far ignoring or dismissing signals and information, we can lose sensitivity to our own bodies.

Protecting Others From Our Feelings

Sometimes we ignore or push away our feelings out of a desire to protect another person. Whenever I visited my dad, eventually the day came when he would take me back home to my mom's house. I would wake up in the morning with a lump in my throat, and I would fight all day to not cry. It wasn't that I didn't want to be with my mom. Since my parents were divorced, I only got to see my dad during school vacations, and I knew I would miss him when we weren't together. I would hold in my feelings and try to distract myself however I could. I didn't want to make my dad feel bad or guilty because I was sad.

Sometimes, in an effort to protect another person from our feelings, we ignore or dismiss *their* feelings and intuition because we don't want to hurt or upset them. This happens a lot to children. If it occurs often with parents or other influential adults, it can cause the child to question their feelings to the point where they lose trust in themselves. It usually looks something like this. Mom is in the kitchen chopping vegetables for the salad, and in walks her daughter. The little girl notices her mother's tense body and furrowed brow, so she asks, "Mommy, what's wrong?"

Mom has had a disagreement with Dad, and she is upset. But it's an adult issue, and she doesn't want her daughter to be concerned about it. If mom says, "Nothing, sweetheart. Everything's fine," as she continues chopping the vegetables, she communicates to her daughter that she's incorrect in sensing that anything was wrong, and the young girl doubts herself.

But, if she responds by saying, "Oh, thanks for asking, sweetheart. I was thinking about something that is bothering me, but it's nothing for you to worry about," she acknowledges the daughter's intuition and reinforces the daughter's ability to trust herself.

Dissociation Due to Trauma

An extreme version of ignoring or dismissing occurs when a person learns to disassociate from their body's input. I've worked with several clients who had a dissociative tendency. In order to not feel overwhelmed by their feelings and emotions, these people would separate themselves from their feelings, and over time, they lost the connection to their bodily sensations and input. For some, it was a coping strategy that resulted because of trauma or abuse. In other cases, the person was very sensitive or empathic and had either grown up in an environment where emotions were not honored, or the person was made to feel wrong for responding to their feelings and expressing their emotions.

Overstimulation

The most widespread issue I see that causes people to lose a connection with their body is desensitization by overstimulation from technology, electricity, mechanical devices, and too much time indoors or in synthetic environments. Urban areas have an inherently high concentration of concrete, asphalt, and metal structures, and this causes the energy in the environment to bounce around and intensify rather than dissipate the way it would in a more natural environment with grass and trees or sand. I've seen the impact of this overstimulation and desensitization in many of the clients I have worked with, and I've learned about it from my own experience.

For seven years, I staffed for the SkyHorseEGE™ certification program at Ariana's ranch, first in Valley Ford, CA, and then in Point Arena, CA. Both of these towns are thirty minutes or more from the nearest city. The course was three weeks long, and it was too far to commute home, so I stayed on Ariana's property. Not only was I in nature, but I was also in the practices of EGE, day in and day out. Away from the city, I could feel my senses and sensitivities softly and subtly open up. I gained a deeper self-awareness and an expanded peripheral awareness. I was listening for subtle changes and shifts in the people, the horses, and the environment. My sense of time shifted to a more relaxed, methodical pace, rather than the fast and frantic pace that is typically felt in a city. All of my senses and my awareness were fully open; my body was like a highly sensitive, finely tuned instrument.

At the end of the three weeks, on my drive home to San Jose, I could feel the intensity of input increase. It came in waves as I drove in and out of rural and urban areas. In the final hour of my drive, the intensity of San Francisco and the Silicon Valley energy field was overwhelming. As I re-entered city life, it felt that the whole world had been hooked up to an amplifier turned up full blast. It was a shock to my system. Cars, people, concrete roads, pavement, houses, buildings, all so close together with no space in between. All of the energy came at me at once. My body felt bombarded. It was like turning on your car and getting blasted by the radio because the last person to drive it had cranked up the volume listening to their favorite song.

Coming home always required an adjustment. At first it was difficult, but after experiencing it several times, I began to understand what was happening, and I took steps to make it easier.

I learned to keep my calendar relatively clear for the first several days I was home. I had to allow my body to adjust, to become desensitized, once again. When we live in cities, we have to allow some degree of desensitization in order to keep from becoming overwhelmed, but if the degree of desensitization is too much, or we lose our awareness or ability to adjust the amplitude, we miss out on the information that our body is processing. In EGE, we have practices that can help manage and adjust to shifts in energy and amplitude.

The body plays a key role in helping us get unstuck, and with all of the information that the body holds and processes, failing to engage the body is a shortfall of many personal development methods. If a person has had a low level of body awareness and connection, or has lost their connection, it is important that any method or practitioner employs a means to help the person regain it. Some psychologists, coaches, teachers, and leaders have come to understand this missing connection, and they have incorporated ways for addressing the body into their work by incorporating *somatics*.

Somatics

The term somatics has various meanings depending on who you ask and the context, and the word somatic gets attached to a lot of other words, which can make it difficult to define. Somatics is fundamental to the philosophy and practice of Equine Guided Education (EGE), so I'd like to take some space here to say a few things about other forms (interpretations) of somatics that are valid, but not necessarily what I'm referring to in the context of EGE, and share the definition that is used in the context of EGE.

The origin of the word somatic comes from the Greek word *soma*, meaning "the body—the physical form distinct from the mind, soul, and spirit," and -*tic* meaning "pertaining to," coming together as "pertaining to the body." While many modern references similarly define somatics as "of the body, relating to or affecting the body," some have adopted a more holistic definition. The Center for Somatic Studies has defined somatics as "the living body in its wholeness" and identifies the soma as a process of doing and being, rather than an abstract entity.[19]

Many forms of somatics focus on the body in a physical, physiological, and tactile way. Examples of these are somatic massage, Rolfing, Feldenkrais Method, and Hanna Somatics, a type of bodywork created by Thomas Hanna who defined somatics as "the body experienced from within." Somatic methods that focus solely on the body are useful for physical issues like relieving pain or rehabbing an injury. The relief or releases brought on by these methods can indirectly benefit our mind, spirit, and soul, but these methods don't address them directly. Other forms of somatics, like somatic coaching and somatic psychology, include the mind, with a focus on how the mind interprets the sensations and physical response of the body.

Two Is Better Than One

Because there is so much going on with our body that does not get processed through the conscious mind, somatic methods that work with the body directly or work with the mind through the body can be more effective than using psychological techniques on the mind alone. When I work somatically to help a client solve a personal problem or make a change, we engage the conversation through body talk—observing the person's posture, where their weight is on their feet when they're standing, their breathing patterns, and other signals. All of these provide clues to their inner state, and allow me to see when their spoken words are incongruent with their body talk.

Sharon, a college student, had taken a semester off school to deal with some health issues. Her health had resolved, but she was struggling to get herself back to school and she wanted help. As she stood in the round pen with Ruby, the horse, she spoke about wanting to go back to school to finish her business degree. As she spoke, she was looking at the ground, her shoulders were slumped, and there was a lack of energy in her voice. I asked her to notice her body and how she was feeling. I shared with her my observation that her posture didn't seem to line up with what she was saying, and it made me wonder if she was saying what she really wanted. I asked if there was something else that she wanted instead.

"I really want to study music," Sharon said softly.

"Okay, then talk to Ruby about that," I replied.

Sharon began to tell Ruby about the kind of music she played and the ideas she had for writing music. This time as she spoke, there were energy and enthusiasm in her voice, she was looking up and her chest was open. It was obvious to all of us watching that when Sharon spoke about music, her words and her body aligned.

The connection between body posture and mood works both ways. In Sharon's case, as she connected to the joy she feels in music, her change in mood caused a change in her body posture. But similarly, changing body posture can influence mood. For example, when you have your arms crossed and all your weight is on your heels, it's difficult to be open to another person's viewpoint. Standing with even weight on your feet, front to back and left to right, with arms relaxed at your side presents a more receptive mood.

Another example of posture influencing mood is that it's harder to stay depressed when you sit up straight with your shoulders back. One morning, I got to witness my daughter apply a similar strategy in her own life. Michaella came into the office to say goodbye before heading to school. She was dressed unusually well, wearing a cute sweater with her pants tucked into her high-heeled boots. Often, she goes to school in sweatpants and a sweatshirt.

My husband asked her why she was all dressed up.

She explained that a few days earlier, her boyfriend had broken up with her, and Michaella said she didn't want to feel down and depressed all day. She knew if she dressed in less casual clothes and shoes that would make her stand upright and feel pretty, she would have a better day. Michaella is a student of EGE and somatics. She has learned that if she is in an undesirable mood, she can shift it by changing her body posture. It warms my heart when I see her put this knowledge into practice.

On a deeper level, working somatically can help us address unresolved trauma held in the body. During a traumatic event, the experience causes a contraction in the body. If the body holds on to the contraction rather than releasing it and returning to a relaxed state, that contraction will cause a block in the flow of energy. This acts as an unresolved trauma. If the flow of energy remains blocked over time, it will cause *dis-ease*—a lack of ease or harmony within the body. This can manifest as physical pain, tension, tight muscles, etc. In some cases, the dis-ease impacts an organ. If left unaddressed, it can eventually manifest as cancer or another life-threatening disease.

All the information the body takes in that does not get processed by the conscious mind stays in the body. According to Dr. Peter A. Levine, who developed Somatic Experiencing™, some people have a bodily memory of trauma, but no conscious memory of it. Through many client sessions, Levine witnessed how clients' bodies told their stories of trauma, even if the clients had no specific memories.[20] This form of somatic practice is used to treat early or severe trauma and Post-traumatic stress disorder.

In the context of Equine Guided Education, somatics is "the art and science of the inter-relational process between awareness, biological function, and environment, all three factors being understood as a synergistic whole: the mind, body, spirit as a unity; the unity of the self," as defined by Ariana Strozzi Mazzucchi.[21] In EGE, we learn to increase our somatic awareness by paying attention to our body, to notice what we are noticing and what changes in our body as we do so. We also pay attention to the energy—of ourselves, of others (horses and people), and of the environment. This attention to the self, others, and environment becomes a practice that helps us balance the amount of input we receive from our mind and take in more information from our senses and intuition.

In EGE, we have a unique somatic practice that includes elements related to the spirit and soul—a focus on intention, a larger sense of purpose and meaning, and a connection to something beyond ourselves.

9

Spirit and Soul

You may be wondering what the difference is between the spirit and the soul. It can be confusing because spirit and soul are sometimes used to define each other, and they are often used interchangeably, creating the impression among many people that they are the same thing, but they are not. All the major spiritual and religious traditions and schools of thought differentiate between the two, and we are going to take a look at how each is defined and described. In the differentiation, we will find clues about how to identify a spiritual crisis, and what makes a crisis of the soul.

Spirit

The English word, spirit, comes from the Latin *spiritus*, meaning "breath" which is distinguished from the Latin *anima*, translated as soul, meaning "to breathe." In Greek, this distinction exists between *pneuma* "breath, motile air, spirit" and *psyche* "soul, to breathe," which we know also has a relationship to the mind. The meaning of the words spirit and soul are so similar, it is easy to see how they have been used interchangeably, and yet, we see in the origin of the words the intent to distinguish them. With *spiritus* and *pneuma* representing the noun *breath*—the air taken into and expelled from the lungs, and *anima* and *psyche* representing the verb *to breathe*—the act of taking in and expelling air from the lungs, we can get a picture of the *spirit as that which is breathed by the soul.* In other words, the soul is animated (made alive) by the act of breathing the breath that is spirit.

To test this concept, I began to search for more distinctions. Modern internet dictionaries were not very helpful because they use characteristics of the spirit to describe the soul and vice versa, so I turned to ancient texts and looked at several different cultural traditions for a deeper understanding of the distinctions.

The Greek word for spirit is used in the Bible to refer to that which gives life to the body. James 2:26 reads, "the body without the spirit (*pneuma*) is dead."[22] The Hebrew word for spirit, *ruach*, meaning wind or breath, appears in Proverbs 18:14, which states, "The human spirit can endure a sick body, but who can bear a crushed spirit?"[23] indicating that while it is the spirit that sustains a person through illness, the spirit of a troubled person can be crushed.

In the Japanese tradition of Shinto, the word *kami* (also *shin* or *jin*) is defined as "god," "spirit," or "spiritual essence," with all these terms meaning "the energy generating a thing." Kami refers to the divinity or sacred essence, the nature of kami that manifests in rocks, trees, rivers, wind, animals, places, and people. It is kami that incites the inspiration, wonder, and sense of awe (sacredness) associated with a place, person, or phenomena.[24] In traditional Chinese culture, *Qi* is the vital force forming part of any living thing. Qi translates literally as "air," and also means "material energy," "life force," or "energy flow." It is the underlying principle in Chinese traditional medicine.[25] In Hindu philosophy, *prana* is the Sanskrit word meaning "primary energy, breath, life force, or vital principle." According to the *Yoga International* article "Understanding Prana" by Dr. David Frawley, "Prana has many levels of meaning, from the physical breath to the energy of consciousness itself. Prana is not only the basic life-force, it is the original creative power. It is the master form of all energy working at every level of our being."[26]

In amalgamation, spirit is the vital force that animates life. It's our energy and vitality, the living force in the body that allows us to continue living. It is the divine spark or light within us, and the source of power for the body and soul. It is the part of us that connects to nature, other beings and spirits, God, Source, the Divine—the interconnectedness of all things. When we die, the spirit leaves the body. Some say the spirit ceases to exist, while the soul moves on.[27] But if energy cannot be created or destroyed, it seems more likely that our energy changes form. Perhaps our spirit is reabsorbed into the flow of cosmic or divine energy, while our soul moves on beyond the earthly plane of existence.

Soul

The English word, soul, has origins in Old English *sawol*, and in Old High German *seula*, which hold that the soul is our non-physical essence.[28] To review, the Greek word for soul is psyche, and the Latin word for soul is anima, both mean "to breathe."

In Hebrew, the word *nephesh* refers to the aspects of sentience, and human beings and animals are both described as having nephesh. In the Bible's Genesis story, it is said that Adam became a living nephesh. Other texts in Hebrew refer to *nepes met*, meaning a dead nephesh, implying nephesh exists whether alive or dead and giving it the quality of being eternal, a trait often associated with concepts of the soul.

The Sanskrit word *Atman* refers to the inner self or soul. In Hindu philosophy, Atman is the first principle, the true self of an individual beyond identification with phenomena, the essence of an individual. Hinduism holds the belief that there is Atman (soul, self) in every being. Within Hinduism is the school of yoga, which holds that there is an individual soul and a universal soul, Atman being the universal soul.

In contrast, Buddhism teaches the doctrine of *anatta* (Pali), or in Sanskrit *anatman*, meaning "no self" or the illusion of self. The belief is that all things are in a constant state of flux, and a human being has no permanent self. While Buddhism does not subscribe to an identity of "I" or "me," it also does not deny an incorporeal component in living things that can continue after death. Some schools of Buddhism have the view that there are three minds (here we see the connection to psyche): *very subtle mind*, which, like the soul, does not disintegrate in death; *subtle mind*, which disintegrates in death and which is the "dreaming mind" or "unconscious mind;" and *gross mind*, which does not exist when one is sleeping. Even though Buddhism doesn't have an exact translation of soul, it mirrors the concept of psyche with characteristics of the very subtle mind.[29]

Distinct from spirit, the soul is who we are, our essence. It's our core, original self, our archetypal nature, which forms our character and personality, yet it transcends our personal sense of identity. Our soul carries the blueprint of our highest potential for our life, our fate and destiny. It's the DNA of our psyche. It is the incorporeal essence of a human being or animal, regarded as immortal.

Concepts of karma, the law of cause and effect, and "you reap what you sow" are connected to the soul. There is individual karma and mass karma, which can affect a group of people, be it a family, a nation, or a planet.[30] The soul carries attributes of the intangible (psychic) aspects of our ancestral heritage which mirror the genetic history held by the cells in the body. This is where we get the concept of "blood memory," when someone feels the impact of past events or the experience of their ancestors as though they themselves experienced it, and the concept of "sins of the fathers," when a younger generation experiences the consequences of the deeds of a previous generation.

Many theories depict the soul as one of many layers of the psyche, along with ego, subconscious mind, shadow, personal unconscious, and collective unconscious. Although the terms may vary from culture to culture, they tend to reflect a progression from lower, mundane states of awareness to higher, more refined states.

Bringing It All Together

The way I see it, our soul incarnates as a human being having a body, mind, and spirit. The spirit is what animates the soul, the mind connects our soul to our body via the brain, the heart, the gut, and other subtle energetic channels, and the body gives form to the soul allowing us to interact on the material plane of earth.

Each aspect of being—body, mind, spirit, and soul—is distinguishable, yet interconnected and inseparable. It's like a rainbow with the distinct colors of red, orange, yellow, green, blue, indigo, and violet. In the rainbow, it is difficult to see where one color ends and the other begins, and it is the same with these various aspects of our being.

Differentiating between characteristics of the spirit and the soul is more challenging than differentiating between the mind and body aspects. When we define the characteristics of the body, we can derive meaning and understanding through observation, feeling, measuring, and tracking its tangible aspects. We can do the same with the mind when it comes to monitoring synapses, neurotransmitters, and hormonal processes. But when we move to the intangible aspects of the mind, the lines get fuzzy, and they are fuzzier still when attempting to define and articulate the more ethereal aspects of spirit and soul.

Metaphors, Myths, and Archetypes

Because their properties and qualities are felt and sensed but impossible to see or to measure, often we do not have exact words to describe spirit and soul, or the qualities that spirit and soul possess. Metaphors, myths, and archetypes can help us to convey meaning and generate understanding of these qualities.

Metaphor

The metaphor gives us a picture or a comparison that helps us recognize the essence of what we are trying to communicate. For example, you've probably heard the phrase "his spirit was broken." You can't see a broken spirit the way you can see a broken leg, so the metaphor helps us grasp the meaning that the person experienced a kind of hurt. If I say, "I put my heart and soul into it," it conveys that I've given my all, and my efforts came from the deepest part of me where meaning originates.

Through the use of metaphors, we can begin to differentiate between spirit and soul, and we can distinguish a spiritual crisis from a crisis of the soul. A *spiritual crisis* has to do with a breakdown in your connection to nature, to others, to yourself, or to God, Source, or the Divine. Without this connection, your energy cannot flow or engage, and the spirit— your life force, Qi, intention—is diminished or restricted from manifesting that which your soul is here to be and do.

A crisis of the soul is often referred to through metaphor as "the dark night of the soul" because it can feel like you are all alone in a dark place. It relates to a collapse in your perceptions of who you are or your perceived meaning of life. It is usually accompanied by a feeling of being "lost" or a loss of purpose. It can feel very lonely, and this can trigger survival fears. It can feel like depression, like nothing makes sense or matters. Sometimes it is triggered by an extreme event like a disaster or the death of someone close to you. It is where you meet your shadow self, your unconscious, your deepest longings that you may have been suppressing.

In the metaphor of the dark night of the soul, something must die for something new to be born. It requires you to let go of, or let *die*, an old set of beliefs or ideals, an old version of you, that now restricts your growth, so you can *birth* a new version of yourself that moves you forward into the next phase of your potential. It is about a need to know and align to the greater *why* that leads you to your highest potential. If you resist what your soul is trying to bring about, it can lead to despair. But if you embrace it, you can emerge with a greater sense of aliveness and purpose and a deeper connection to yourself and what has meaning in your life.

Myths and Archetypes

Myths are traditional or legendary stories. These stories might be accepted in certain circles as true, or they may be known to be made-up. Either way, they are used to explain ideas about how the world works and how people act in it. Myths are usually centered around a being, hero, or event that explains some natural or social phenomenon. Greek and Roman mythology bring us stories of ancient gods and goddesses, like Zeus, Athena, Neptune, and Venus, waging war and playing tricks on each other. The stories of Abraham and Isaac, Moses and the Ten Commandments, and Noah's ark are also examples of ancient stories told again and again to explain why some things are the way they are, while conveying life lessons of faith, hope, and trust in God.

The main characters in myths represent archetypes. Archetype means original pattern. It comes from the Greek words *archein*, which means "original or old" and *typos*, which means "pattern, model, or type." Archetypes represent psychological and emotional patterns within the human psyche.

The psychologist, Carl Jung, used the concept of archetypes in his theories. He believed archetypes are inherited patterns of thought that emerge out of the past experience of the whole race since its beginning, and are present in our unconscious minds. Some archetypes are global—father, mother, rebel, orphan, rescuer, victim, artist, etc., and others are cultural—king, chief, emperor, leader, explorer, pilgrim, innovator, and entrepreneur. Some are ancient—the Hindu deities like Vishnu, Shiva, and Ganesha, Greek and Roman gods like Poseidon, Hera, Jupiter, and Mercury, and some are modern—the computer geek, the undercover agent, and the boogeyman.

Using archetypes helps give us a language to understand, explain, and describe aspects of the soul's experience. When I work with someone, I look for unconscious, repetitive patterns that may be contributing to keeping them stuck. An understanding of archetypes has helped me to better identify patterns and themes, and given me a context to help the person relate to and work with their pattern. The name of an archetype contains within it a host of descriptors that connect it to an associated pattern.

Let's look at the damsel. The damsel archetype instantly conjures up a clear, detailed image of a young, unmarried woman, usually of some level of nobility. Because of her youth, she may be naive or inexperienced. Because of her nobility, she may be accustomed to having things done for her rather than learning or knowing how to do things for herself.

A well-known pattern of the damsel archetype is "damsel in distress." This repetitive pattern tells of a helpless woman getting herself into trouble or finding herself in a difficult situation and needing someone else, usually a man (a knight in shining armor), to come to her aid. The damsel may be naive to the complexity of her situation, and she may feel entitled to the aid she seeks. When the knight rescues the damsel, there is a sense of satisfaction for both parties, which often leads to romantic involvement, but this distress-rescue pattern rarely sustains a long-term romantic relationship, so the damsel repeats the pattern with the next knight who comes along. When the damsel is in trouble, if no one shows up to help get her out of it, she may become overwhelmed, resentful, or depressed.

To get out of the loop of this pattern, a person living out the damsel in distress archetype must choose a different response to replace it. She must first recognize when she is in a situation where she is looking for someone else to fix her problem, and then she must choose instead to pull from the resources within herself to become her own rescuer. By breaking out of the repetitive pattern, she transitions into the still feminine damsel without the distress pattern, and she moves toward the maturity of a dame or a queen.

Studying archetypes has helped me better identify the patterns and universal themes that influence my own life, as well as my clients'. Caroline Myss uses this concept of core archetypes in her book *Sacred Contracts*, where she addresses aspects of the soul. According to Myss, your Sacred Contract is "the guided plan for your life." It's your soul contract. Prior to birth, your soul makes an agreement to meet and work with certain people, in certain places, at certain times during the course of your life, and each soul has their own set of twelve core archetypes that play a role in the unfolding of the Sacred Contract. Other archetypal patterns influence you at different times, but the twelve core archetypes are always with you.[31]

One of my core archetypes is the "mediator." Most of the time, my mediator archetype is an asset. It helps me see and respect both sides of a situation or conflict and gives me a knack for finding balance or agreement. It helps me communicate with others in a way that helps me understand their point of view, even if it is quite different than my own. This is beneficial when I'm working with clients, and it also comes in handy when I'm working on a team. If there are any misunderstandings or disagreements, I can usually help both sides come together to see the other's point of view more objectively, without taking the disagreement or misunderstanding personally, while finding a workable solution.

But if I don't manage this mediator pattern, it can get me into trouble, like when my husband and one of my children have a misunderstanding or disagreement. I don't like when there is conflict at home, and my mediator pattern will make me want to rush in and help them resolve it, but if I am always doing this, they don't learn to mediate for themselves. It is important for me to recognize when it's not my role or responsibility to mediate, and let the other parties find their own solution.

Religion and Astrology

Two tools people have used for ages to understand and address the spirit and soul are religion and astrology. In addition to giving us a language to talk about spirit and soul, they provide more direct counsel and methodologies for dealing with these aspects.

Religion

Often when we talk about issues of the spirit or soul, the conversation leads to someone bringing up religion, whether we intended to address religion or not. Modern advice suggests we steer clear of religion and politics, but sometimes engaging in difficult and touchy topics is necessary to help people get unstuck.

When it comes to navigating issues of the spirit or soul, many people turn to religion for guidance. They might reference a sacred text or call on a pastor, priest, or other spiritual leader for insights and prayer, or they might visit a sacred site or temple to perform a ritual such as lighting a candle or meditating.

Historically, spirituality was pursued by the very religious who desired to engage with religion in a deeper, more personal way. But in my work, I've seen an increasing trend toward people wanting to pursue spirituality, to deepen their sense of connectedness to the divine in a way that is not religious, and when the topic of spirit comes up, it has been necessary to acknowledge that while spirituality can be religious, it doesn't have to be.

A 2017 study showed the percentage of US adults who consider themselves to be "spiritual, but *not* religious" had increased by 8% in five years to over a quarter of the population (27%). In accordance with this study, today's spirituality has taken on a broader definition. Some consider spirituality to be the personal pursuit of the sacred (God, the Divine, Source) and for others, it simply refers to a deeper pursuit of "meaning."[32]

Many people today who engage in spirituality feel the need to emphasize that they are not religious. This may be because religion, which tends to incorporate public rituals and organized doctrines, has recently become associated with unfortunate connotations of moralism, piety, and hypocrisy. These connotations are in part a result of the uncovering by the media of widespread sexual abuse by priests and pastors, and religious extremists committing terrorism.

Another factor, not as publicized, that contributes to the negative connotations many people have about religion is the spiritual abuse that occurs inside of organized religion and religious institutions. Spiritual abuse, in this context, happens when spiritual authority or spiritual means are used to demean, manipulate, control, or exploit someone, and when an authority figure, such as a pastor, priest, or guru seeks to control individuals and ensure obedience. It's a power-centered abuse that occurs where there is an experience of the sacred, and someone uses their power within the framework of spiritual belief to satisfy their own needs at the expense of others. We tend to think of this happening within cults, but a simple internet search reveals blogs, support groups, and therapy resources for sufferers spanning most major religious traditions.[33]

While religion is not the only context for spiritual abuse, it's a major one. In her *Psychology Today* article "Therapy and Spiritual Abuse," Andrea Mathews, LPC, NCC, writes:

"Spiritual abuse is abuse of another human being's spirit—the deeper essential *Me-ness* of me—sometimes referred to as the soul or the authentic Self. Spiritual abuse can happen at home, at the hands of parents, who are our first gods. It can happen in school, perpetrated by teachers or other authority figures. And it can happen in churches, temples, mosques, and synagogues—also perpetrated by authority figures, who seem to represent the divine. It happens more frequently in homes and places of worship, ritual, and prayer. But it happens anywhere where we are vulnerable to the influence of another person, who might misuse that influence, either consciously or unconsciously, to define us.

As a result of spiritual abuse, a person can become spiritually wounded causing damage to their personal relationship with God or their sacred practice. This type of wounding tends to affect a person's ability to trust others, as well as themselves. It can deeply damage one's sense of self and self-esteem. Some people are unable to separate their sacred beliefs from the abuse, and this can cause them to entirely distrust God or any spiritual pursuit.

A person may know she has been spiritually abused when she has been taught, either covertly or overtly, to negate her own original thoughts, emotions, beliefs and body sensations because she has been convinced in some way that to operate out of these would be a betrayal of a sacred contract with either the divine, the divine's representative or a parent."[34]

I've experienced spiritual abuse first hand, so I understand the challenges of re-engaging with religion and the difficulty of redeveloping trust once it's been broken. For those who have been wounded by dogmatic, legalistic, and fundamentalist theologies and the spiritual abuse that often accompanies these, it is imperative to find a safe place to heal and an alternative way of tending to the needs of the spirit and soul. For me, and many people I've worked with, EGE has provided this space and opportunity.

While religion is supposed to help with spiritual issues, it can also create them. How then do we address matters of the spirit or a spiritual crisis? Can we have spirituality without religion? Can we have religion without dogma or the need to control others' behavior in the name of God?

The root word of "religion" comes from the Latin *religio* meaning "to reconnect" or "bind back to" referring to the innate impulse in human beings to connect to the source from which life springs.[35] And it is this impulse that drives the pursuit of spirituality. If we take the original meaning and intention of religion, whether *Eastern*— Hinduism, Buddhism, Taoism, Confucianism or *Western*—Islam, Christianity, Judaism we can see religion's influence in the practices guiding the pursuit of spirituality, be it through prayer, meditation, ritual, or pilgrimage. By the definition of religion in its original sense, I don't believe we can pursue spirituality without it touching on some aspect of religion, but I do believe we can pursue spirituality without being religious. We can engage our spiritual practices in a private and individual way that does not require participation in an organized religion and is not confined within the walls of a church or temple. Some of my most profound spiritual experiences have been outdoors in the presence of horses.

Astrology

Astrology has close ties with ancient religion, and it is one of the oldest tools for addressing the soul. According to Sid Jefferies' article on his Facts Behind Faith website "Astrology was the foundation of all the ancient faiths: Egyptian, Babylonian, Greek, Roman, Zoroastrian, Mithraism, the Druids and the Norse gods… Astrology was also at the heart of the Mayan, Aztec and Inca religions in the Americas with the Sun as supreme God."[36] When we look at all religions and the calendars we use, the days of the week, the months of the year, and the seasons, it is all based on astrology.

But just like the other philosophies and methodologies we've looked into, astrology has gone through an evolution through the ages, and not all views of astrology are the same. In ancient times, many civilizations worshiped the stars and planets. The medieval view of astrology holds that the stars and planets influence things such as the weather, the growth of crops, and even the personalities of babies being born. This view is associated with what we see today in the trite, daily, sun-sign horoscopes and in the practice of fortune-telling. These views of astrology contribute to the negative connotations it holds today.

Astrology has long been considered sacrilegious in many faith-based communities, especially Christianity. In my opinion, this is due to associations with ancient and medieval views and a misunderstanding of what astrology is and is not. Personally, I have found some astrology models helpful. Human life is made of cycles and seasons, and astrology can help us recognize what is coming so we can be better prepared. The signs of the zodiac represent archetypes and the houses of the zodiac represent archetypal patterns of human development. I have worked with interpretations of my birth chart through intuitive-archetypal astrology, and I have found that using these symbolic archetypes, archetypal patterns, and relationships to gain insight into the self is more informative and accurate than any personality test or assessment I've taken.

The philosophy of Intuitive-Archetypal Astrology, as defined by Robert Ohotto, postulates that as souls on earth at this time, we are connected to the energetic and creative cycles of Planet Earth. These cycles are archetypically woven into Earth's time and space, and we are individually, culturally, and collectively subject to current cycles and themes, such as global shifts in climate patterns, the impact of natural disasters, economic changes, etc. The cycles of the stars and planets mirror the "energetic/psychic weather patterns" of Earth.[37] By tracking these cycles, we can become more aware of what energies are at play during a given season and take a more proactive role in how we engage with the opportunities they bring. The symbolic sight of this philosophy does not attempt to predict the future, but rather it offers a blueprint of coordinates that holds the potential for various outcomes. When we face a dilemma, or we are at a crossroads, understanding which themes are currently activated can lead us to asking better questions and engaging in a more focused inquiry. Whether we take notice and use this available information to develop ourselves, or we ignore it and let life happen to us, it is our choice.

Astrology, just like any tool or method, has the potential to be used in a helpful or harmful way. Some astrologists still practice medieval forms and offer fortune-telling services that prey on the uneducated who are simply experiencing a period of uncertainty and looking for help. The mere suggestion that a future event will unfold in a certain way can influence how you think about it, and therefore, its potential impact on your life, so allowing someone to tell you your future is a slippery slope.

Anytime we give someone permission to speak into our life, we make ourselves vulnerable to their influence. The same applies to therapists, coaches, pastors, teachers, etc.

Choosing a practitioner to work with is an important decision. I believe it is essential to filter the input we allow into our lives. Whatever tools or methods we engage to address our spirit and soul, it should be done with care. The same goes with our body and mind. I encourage you to do some research and get to know the background of any practitioner or methodology you decide to engage. Make sure they honor you as an individual and respect the complexity of the relationship of your interconnected body, mind, spirit, and soul. It often takes a multifaceted approach and the ability to address multiple aspects simultaneously to initiate a breakthrough.

PART 3:

Getting Unstuck

10

Change and the Power of Choice

Get ready to take the reins back into your own hands. In part one, we looked at the way your beliefs, fears, and habits are interconnected and can keep you feeling stuck. In part two, we explored the complexity of the integrated aspects of your being—body, mind, spirit, and soul. We looked at some of the tools and modalities that can be useful in addressing each aspect, and I shared my experience with what has worked for me and the importance of taking an integrated approach, acknowledging all aspects of the self.

Now, I am going to share a truth that is the key to getting unstuck. Embracing this truth and following where it leads will put the reins back in your hands. Are you ready?

The truth is this: You are not really stuck.

Wait . . . what?

You aren't really stuck. You can't be stuck. Time and life move on. Things change. People change. The world around us changes. Even if you wanted to, you couldn't keep things from shifting and changing. If you are *feeling* stuck, it is because you are resisting change or avoiding making a choice. You can stop *feeling* stuck by embracing change and exercising the power of choice in your life.

Embracing Change

When I think about change, these words roll in my head: Life's about change, nothing stays the same. Change is inevitable. Children age and mature. Family members pass on. A business closes. Jobs are lost, and new ones are found. Fires, hurricanes, and earthquakes tear down homes and towns. Structures are rebuilt, and new services are sourced. Many changes occur that cannot be prevented or controlled. Sometimes, we can see them coming and prepare, and sometimes they happen unexpectedly.

In the course of life, a significant change occurs, on average, every four to seven years. In general, we enter school around five years old, and we transition between elementary, middle, and high school. College lasts four to six years for most. In the trades, three to five years of work is required as an apprentice before one can test to become a journeyman, and usually another four years as a journeyman is required to become a master. There's the "seven-year itch," a common point of stress in many marriages. Just count by seven and think what changed for you around the age of seven, fourteen, twenty-one, twenty-eight, thirty-five, and so on.

Navigating change is inherent in the cycle of human development, and it goes like this: experience, learn, integrate, repeat. With each experience we learn something new, or something we previously learned is reinforced so that it has a deeper context. Then we integrate that learning into our perspective, perception, and understanding for use in the next experience. This process influences how we relate to ourselves, how we relate to others, and how we relate to the world—our environment and communities—as we continue on our journey to the next change.

Change is a catalyst that can push you toward personal growth and development. And as a human being wired for survival, you have internal resources to aid you in making these changes—your mind, creativity and intellect, energy and will, intuition, and your ability to learn new skills and use tools. It is through the experience of change that you learn, adapt, and develop resilience.

Changes can seem big or small, easy or difficult. Some are imposed on us, and others come as the result of choices we made, consciously or unconsciously. Changes are commonly categorized as internal—primarily within the psyche as in thoughts and feelings, or external—tangible and visible like a haircut, but in reality, any internal change will cause an external change and vice versa. Internal and external changes are interconnected and interdependent.

While an external change may seem like a big deal because it is immediately obvious, internal changes are often more powerful, like a secret weapon. A tiny internal shift has the potential to initiate a quantum level transformation. It may or may not be big or immediately obvious to others, but it can change everything about your life and how you experience it.

This happened for Kathy on the final day of a group EGE workshop. On Sunday afternoon, when Kathy entered the round pen with Cari, the horse, she expressed her frustration with growing her business. She was attending networking functions, placing ads, and putting up flyers. In all cases, Kathy was addressing the challenges of educating people who didn't know what Hanna Somatics was and trying to convince them that it could help them. Before becoming certified in Hanna Somatics, Kathy spent twenty-four years in the tech industry gaining success in her role as vice president of marketing. Marketing was her thing. She had been applying the same marketing techniques that worked for her in the tech industry to her new business, but it wasn't working.

"Instead of focusing on clients who don't understand your work and convincing them that they need it, what if you focused on attracting clients who are already familiar with somatics, or are already searching for a better alternative?" I asked.

"Wow," Kathy replied. "I never considered that I could ask the universe to send me the clients I want. Could it be that simple?"

"Try it on. Imagine that Cari is a client and see if you can get her to connect and walk with you," I replied.

As Kathy began to embody her new intention, her energy shifted. Rather than projecting her energy out, as in her efforts to educate people, her energy became lighter, softer, and more inviting. Cari became interested in Kathy and began to follow her around the pen. Kathy had a visceral experience of this new energy, this new way of being, as Cari walked freely beside her.

The next day was Monday. At nine o'clock that morning, Kathy received a call from a woman who had already read about Hanna Somatics and was ready to book an appointment. She received several similar calls in the following weeks from new clients who also were ready to book a session, with no need for education or convincing. Within a few months, Kathy's internal change created an external shift that doubled her monthly client sessions, and the increase continued for two years.

Change requires us to walk a different path, to try something new, and this requires courage. Kathy took the courageous step to let go of her old approach in order to try a new way. She embraced change, but many people resist it. They hold on to the past, to "the way things were," not because the new way is bad, nor because the past was all that great. They hold on because the past is what they're used to. They crave the familiar because it is comfortable, even when it is not what they say they want. Change makes us uncomfortable because it is unfamiliar, and this discomfort often causes resistance, which causes suffering. To paraphrase the second noble truth of Buddhism, clinging to that which changes is the definition of suffering. Old beliefs, unproductive habits, and fears can also contribute to resistance, and where resistance persists, people feel stuck.

Another main reason people resist change is the lack of support from those close to them. If you've been having trouble making a change, in addition to your own resistance, you may be experiencing resistance from the people around you. The people closest to you are accustomed to the way you have been, and when you start to change, you become less predictable, which makes you seem less familiar. Your friend or family member might say, "I don't know who you are anymore." The shift to this unfamiliar version of you can result in discomfort and insecurity in your relationship. This person may react to your changes by being unsupportive, resistant, or even defensive. For this reason and more, it's a good idea to enlist a coach or mentor who can support you as you move through significant shifts.

Adapting to an unexpected or unwanted change can be particularly difficult. You may have been the victim of a crime, a natural disaster, an accident, or some other unfavorable situation, and something inside you wants to go back to the way things were before. But you are forever changed by what happened, and you cannot go back. Situations like this can shake your sense of security and contribute to your feeling of powerlessness. While you may have been powerless in preventing the situation or event, you are not powerless in choosing your response. You don't have to remain a victim. You have an opportunity to integrate your experience in a way that serves you.

Recognizing that you are in a change and choosing to engage in it consciously is a necessary step to getting unstuck. Conscious choice allows us to choose a response rather than blindly react.

The Power of Choice

Every day we are met with thousands of choices. But we often don't recognize the opportunity to choose because we unconsciously allow our habits and conditioning to control our actions. We're on autopilot, functioning with pre-programed patterns. As long as things in our external environment and our health remain static, autopilot directs us fairly well. But what happens when we hit a bump, when something changes or shifts, when the flow is interrupted, or when what we've been doing stops working?

If you keep autopilot engaged, you will find yourself reacting rather than responding. In the context of human behavior, reacting is unconscious, and your next action comes from an impulsive, reflexive, or emotionally triggered place, without prior thought or consideration. When you respond consciously you may feel an impulse, reflexive urge, or emotional trigger, but you don't act on it unconsciously. Instead, you pause, letting the feeling move through you. You note the emotions that are coming up, and then you take a big picture look, giving thought and consideration to what is happening, who is present, what you want to take care of, and your desired outcome. From that place, you choose the next action that best serves the situation. You choose a conscious response.

What it comes down to is a question my mentor, Ariana Strozzi Mazzucchi, is famous for asking: *"Are you leading your life, or is it leading you?"*

Read that again.

If you're running on autopilot, if you're allowing circumstances to elicit a reaction, if you're letting what other people think dictate how your life is turning out, then your life is leading you. You're like a boat in the water that is blown this way or that by the wind and carried off in the direction of the current. In contrast, to *lead your life* means you are navigating your way, making conscious choices to raise or lower your sails, to engage the motor and the rudder to influence your direction and speed. You can't remove the winds and the currents in your life, but you can learn how to work with their qualities to reduce resistance and increase propulsion in the direction you wish to go.

Wayne Dyer said, "Our lives are a sum total of the choices we have made." This applies whether your choices were made consciously or unconsciously. Taking responsibility for your choices can be a hard pill to swallow, but it is a necessary step toward leading your life. Feeling stuck comes from being in a constant state of reactivity, tossed about by what others think and confined by the circumstances around you. Remaining in a victim mindset and blaming others or circumstances for the things in your life that are not working out won't free you from feeling stuck. Remember, even if you were victimized by an event or another person, **you** get to decide what you will do next, and how the next chapter of your story is written. Freedom comes through exercising your free will . . . your power of choice.

This is your one life, and your time is limited. It's up to you to define who you are and how you will spend the rest of it. This call to accept self-responsibility is where the rubber meets the road. Yes, it's where the friction is. But you need friction to gain forward movement. Most people resist this call. Rather than step up and lead their own life, they deflect or defer their choices in an attempt to avoid responsibility, and the anxiety that accompanies it. They would rather exist inside self-imposed limitations, thereby limiting the anxiety they experience, instead of meeting life head on and fulfilling their potential. Answering this call to accept self-responsibility means mustering up the courage required to bear the anxiety and taking up the reins to set the direction for your life.

But that's not all. Anxiety is not the only thing that fuels our resistance to choosing. According to philosopher Peter Koestenbaum, all significant decisions, whether personal or organizational, require a commitment to face the anxiety, as well as the guilt and uncertainty that inevitably come with choosing.[38] In working with my clients and in my own life, I have repeatedly seen and experienced the significant challenges of anxiety, guilt, and uncertainty, and the barriers they create when exercising the power of choice and moving through change. Let's take a closer look at each one and explore some strategies for overcoming them.

Anxiety

Before we label and interpret them, emotions are simply energetic information. What's the energy of anxiety before it gets identified? For me, it feels like a swirl of increasing energy spinning between my heart and my gut, and most of the time it is accompanied by a feeling of butterflies in my stomach. If you think in terms of chakras, I would correlate the location of this feeling with both my heart chakra and my solar plexus.

The first time I really examined the energetics of anxiety for myself, I found it difficult to identify a difference in the energetic sensation of anxiety and excitement. I noticed that my interpretation was based on my attitude about the situation in which the sensation occurred. If it was a situation that I presupposed would have a favorable outcome, I interpreted the feeling as excitement, but if I presupposed that the situation would have an unfavorable outcome, or I wasn't sure, I interpreted it as anxiety. Most people seem to interpret anxiety as bad or negative and something they prefer to avoid.

It is our historic associations and conditioned interpretations that cause us to qualify an emotion as good or bad, positive or negative. But before negative associations and interpretations are attached to it, anxiety is simply energy, and if you allow yourself to explore it, you might find, as I have, a new way of looking at anxiety.

This alternate view comes from Koestenbaum, which he attributes to the work of Søren Kierkegaard, a Danish philosopher who did extensive analysis on anxiety. According to Koestenbaum, "anxiety is the experience of growth."[39] And I agree. When you think about it, any time we move from one stage to another, or one effort to the next, we feel anxious.

In other words, the fact that you feel anxious means you are alive. Your spirit, life force, qi, that which animates you has been stirred and summoned, and you are free to choose. You are being asked to make a decision and take action. If you are ready to make a change in your life, take this opportunity to re-examine your relationship with anxiety, and use the energy of it to propel you forward by exercising your power of choice.

Guilt

Anytime you say yes to one thing, you're probably saying no to a bunch of other things, and what often follows is the guilt that comes with choosing. Many people resist making choices to avoid this feeling. I know I have done it; when one child has a sports game and the other has a dance performance at the same time, and I have to decide which to attend. Avoiding choice is also a choice, and it, too, can make you feel guilty. The truth is, guilt can show up regardless of what you choose because you could have chosen differently. It's a paradox. You can't escape the guilt. Koestenbaum says that guilt isn't a result of making the wrong choice, but of the act of choosing itself.

The guilt that comes with choosing can mean you feel damned if you do, and damned if you don't. In the fall of 2016, Achille and I planned a trip to Italy with our three children. We had been dreaming of this trip for several years, and the actual planning and booking of flights and lodging had been over a year in the making. A few weeks before we were scheduled to depart, we encountered some behavior issues with our oldest daughter, Kali. She was 20, attending college.

We had certain expectations because she was still living under our roof, such as if you're not coming home, let us know ahead of time, and keep your room tidy. They weren't extreme, but she had a hard time complying with our requests.

A couple of weeks before the trip, Kali's lack of consideration, on top of previous incidents, made Achille so upset he said he no longer wanted to take her to Italy. He knew I was not as upset as he was, and he knew I wouldn't merely agree, so he made it *my* decision. He didn't want Kali to go, but he wanted it to be my choice. If I chose to have her go, I was going against his wishes, and whatever irritation he experienced during the trip would be my fault. I knew that the intensity of his irritation could ruin the trip, and I didn't like the odds. But then there was the impact of not taking Kali. When I had dreamed of this family trip, I always pictured all five of us on the trip together. Also, how would it impact Kali's feelings of inclusion in the family if we left her out of the trip? I understood that Kali was at the age of individuating herself, which is a natural phase of development that often causes tension between parents and their young adult children. I knew the growing pains were unavoidable, and I didn't want to let them put a wedge between us. It was a dilemma, and I had several sleepless nights while grappling with the decision.

Another week passed, and some mail arrived that indicated Kali's finances were out of order. She'd overdrawn her bank account, and she was past due on her phone bill. Not shocking for a young person trying to figure things out. In my younger years, I'd made similar mistakes. I had attempted, on prior occasions, to teach Kali financial management skills, but as with many young adults, she was not interested in her parents' help or input. Kali tried to sidestep her phone bill by switching phone companies, but it didn't work. With less than a week before our departure, it became clear that her financial debt was over $900. As a financially responsible person wanting to set a good example, I could not, in good conscience, let Kali take a three-and-a-half-week vacation when she was over $900 in debt. I felt she needed to stay home and work to earn the money to pay off her debt.

We had had several interim conversations with Kali about her situation, but the day came when we needed to make a final decision. The more Achille thought about Kali not going, the harder it got for him. Both of us were concerned about the awkwardness we'd feel once we returned. We imagined that anytime we talked about our experiences and fun times from the trip, our other two children would be able to chime in, and Kali would feel left out. Neither of us liked how this made us feel.

During our conversation with Kali, I could feel Achille leaning toward taking her on the trip. When it came down to feeling the impact of actually leaving her home, it was too painful for him. But each time I thought about taking her, I felt my heart and throat tighten up. My body felt resistant to the idea of bringing her on the trip. In the end, I listened to my body, and I held the line. My choice wasn't without anxiety or guilt, but I made the choice that best aligned with the values and beliefs that I hold, that we both hold, and that I felt would set the best example for my daughter to be responsible. I gave Achille the choice to veto my decision, but in spite of his discomfort, he let my decision stand.

Ironically, missing out on the trip did not seem as disappointing for Kali as it was for Achille and me. She wanted to see Italy, but she didn't necessarily want to be with her parents and away from her friends for three and a half weeks. Even today, when I reflect on the decision to not take Kali to Italy, I still feel like it was the best one, not based on the decision itself but based on how I came to it.

Uncertainty

Making choices would be so much easier if we knew the outcome before we had to decide, but that's not the way life works. Many of us hesitate because we are looking for certainty that will never come. So how do we proceed? Tony Schwartz, author of *The Way We're Working Isn't Working*, advises that we abandon our quest for certainty and instead seek a state of openness and curiosity.[40]

If we are certain, then it's already decided, and we're not as open to new ideas and perspectives, and we're not curious about new possibilities beyond our current awareness. I've found openness and curiosity to be two important keys for navigating change in my own life, and in facilitating my clients through their change process. Adopting a state of openness and curiosity creates a mood conducive to growth and learning which contributes to getting unstuck.

Attitude – Your Ace in the Hole

In all cases, you have an ace in the hole—your attitude. Your ultimate power is that you are always free to choose your attitude. No one else can choose it for you. Your attitude colors and drives your story. You are the author, and you get to choose how you interpret what is happening and how you will respond to it. The end of your story is not yet written. If you don't like where your story is headed, the internal change of a new attitude can shift your trajectory.

A prevalent attitude of people who feel stuck comes with the story that "it's just the way it is" or "there's no way out, no other option." It is common in families that children or young adults set out on a path designed for them by someone else, and it can seem as if they have no choice. Perhaps you were conditioned by your culture with some expectation of who you should be and what you should do, with no apparent alternative. Perhaps you've found yourself unhappy and dissatisfied because the path you're on feels like a detour, but you can't justify changing it because you're successful at what you are doing.

I don't believe in zero options or no way out. These ideas are constricting, and they cause irritation that stirs me up, and my core screams, "NO!" The drive to find solutions is hard-wired into me, and it's a big part of what inspires my EGE work. If you are open, if you allow curiosity, you will find a possibility you didn't see before. You may not be able to forgo the anxiety, guilt, and uncertainty, but you can work through them. You may not be able to make everyone happy, but you can find a solution you can live with.

Whatever resistance you may feel toward change and choice, the good news is that you are not truly stuck; it only feels like it. There is a way out. It may be by choosing a new direction, or an alternative interpretation, and it may be through choosing a different attitude. I know . . . easier said than done. But if you allow openness and curiosity, you will discover new possibilities and perspectives you have not yet considered. The answer is already inside of you waiting to be discovered. As Marcus Aurelius said, "If you are distressed by anything external, the pain is not due to the thing itself, but to your estimate of it; and this you have the power to revoke at any moment." Choosing powerfully begins with healing from the inside out and connecting to your internal compass. And that is what we will explore next.

11

Your Internal Guidance System

You were born with an internal guidance system. This system includes resources that are hard-wired at birth, your internal compass, and other aspects that develop as you grow and experience life. Your body, mind, spirit, and soul all have components connected to your internal guidance system, and any lack of integration of any one aspect will impair the system's function.

Your internal compass is your soul, including both the personal and impersonal (eternal) aspects, and certain elements of your intuition. It is the principle component of your internal guidance system. It holds the coordinates of your highest potential, and it is always directing you toward them.

The aspects of your internal guidance system that can be developed include somatic awareness and cognitive functions such as imagination, memory, reasoning, and intuition. Attunement to your internal guidance system goes hand in hand with a healthy self-esteem, which includes the capacity for self-responsibility and trusting yourself.

As with any system, if one element gets out of alignment or disconnected, the system cannot function properly, and outcomes will not be optimal. If you are having trouble making a change or a significant decision, and it has led to feeling stuck, consider it like a warning light on your dashboard signaling that there's a breakdown in your internal guidance system.

Inevitably, we experience conflicts and challenges in life that cause us to pull back or withdraw, and in so doing we diminish, restrict, or retract the energy that flows through our body. For example, experiencing the break-up of a relationship can cause an initial reaction of pulling back to isolate ourselves or withholding our emotions. This energetic contraction is a normal response to conflict and pain. It may take some time to process our feelings, and that is also normal. As long as we move through the process, eventually allowing our energy and emotions to flow and re-engage in life, our system returns to balance. However, if the contraction of energy is held over time because we continue to withhold our feelings and energetic expression, we will begin to drift out of alignment with our internal compass.

An extreme energetic contraction occurs any time we are wounded. Wounds that are left unresolved and unacknowledged can grow and fester, sometimes without our awareness. This holds true for all types of wounding, whether to the body, psyche, or spirit.

Unresolved wounds create an energetic block that, over time, can cause disease. In her book *The Creation of Health*, Caroline Myss shared her experience as a medical intuitive. In collaboration with C. Norman Shealy, M.D., Ph.D., she performed thousands of readings on patients, and she began to identify how a patient's blocked energy manifests as an emotional disorder or physical disease. Myss states "your biography becomes your biology," which I interpret to mean your body is evolving moment by moment in response to your thoughts, beliefs, experiences, and your interpretations of your experiences. Studying her work has helped me understand how the flow of our life force and energy is linked to our emotional and physical well-being and the importance of addressing the problems that cause energetic blocks and restrictions.[41]

Some wounds become particularly deep and debilitating if not addressed. Wounds that result from toxic stress at critical stages during childhood development may cause incomplete development, inhibiting us from recognizing and fulfilling our potential, and lead to disease in adulthood. According to the American Academy of Pediatrics, experiences of extreme adversity, such as prolonged poverty, abuse, or neglect, parental substance abuse or mental illness, and exposure to violence, cause toxic stress and have a negative effect on emerging brain architecture and long-term health. The disruptive impacts of toxic stress caused in early childhood can lead to impairments in learning, behavior, and both physical and mental well-being. Research on this topic suggests that many adult diseases should be viewed as developmental disorders that begin early in life and could be reduced by the alleviation of toxic stress in childhood.[42]

Of course, alleviating all stress in childhood would be ideal, but when we are past prevention as a strategy, the ability to heal still exists. At any stage, healing, improvement, and transformation are possible when a person is fully committed to their self-development and pursuit of health.

Wounds occurring as a direct result of expressing our uniqueness can have a devastating impact on self-esteem. This means someone says or does something that makes you feel wrong for being your authentic self. The degree of impact will depend on the influence that person has in your life. If you were a child, and you were made to feel wrong by a parent or other influential adult, it may have caused you to withdraw or try to be someone other than yourself. Usually, when others judge you as wrong for being yourself, it is because whatever you are doing presses on their own insecurities or feelings of inadequacy, but it is difficult to see this when it's happening, especially for children.

Victim consciousness and a low self-esteem can cause a breakdown in our ability to connect to and follow our internal compass. With victim consciousness, a person refuses to take self-responsibility and instead projects their power outward, blaming others or circumstances for what is not working out. In cases of low self-esteem, one's value is not founded on self-acceptance but rather on what other people think, and the level of acceptance from others.

Social media exacerbates low self-esteem when people project images of who they think they should be in order to find acceptance. It doesn't matter if the person experiences rejection or acceptance, self-esteem is diminished. When there's rejection, the result is obvious. With regards to acceptance, self-esteem is compromised because the acceptance is based on a false image, which only contributes to a feeling that the true self is not enough. Low self-esteem creates insecurity around the social instinct to produce value, to be valued, and to contribute to the whole. Without this sense of value, a person's fear of rejection is triggered because rejection could lead to ostracization and being alone, pressing on the deepest biological fear of a social animal.

Low self-esteem leads some to abandon their sense of self. If you abandon yourself because of what others think, or your developmental process was incomplete, you may end up feeling lost and disconnected from your internal compass. Your entire being seeks alignment, so when there is a disconnect your spirit goes to work to bring it to your attention. It wants you to find the wound or the breakdown, to acknowledge it, and grow through it, allowing the experience to be integrated, and alignment restored. If you do not heed the messages from your internal guidance system, you may start to experience a breakdown in your external environment. This can show up as financial hardship, relationship difficulties, physical illness, or some type of crisis. The more you ignore or resist, the more difficult your situation can become as your spirit will turn up the volume to get your attention.

But you have the ability to heal yourself and your life. Balance and alignment can be restored. The power to heal oneself is inherent in each person. By bringing awareness to any wound and where it originated, you will recognize the patterns and perceptions you have developed as a result, and by changing unproductive patterns and shifting your perspective, you will begin to heal yourself from the inside out. The remedy is to reframe your sense of value, to embrace the truth that you are enough just as you are, and to focus on what is right about you. The process of nurturing your self-esteem is the same one that reconnects you to your internal guidance system, leading to the clarity of purpose and flow that contribute to satisfaction.

Clarity of Purpose

When we find ourselves contemplating questions like *Who am I? Why am I here? What's my purpose?*, it is likely we are feeling disconnected from our internal compass. But these are insufficient questions. The questions we are really searching to answer are these:

Why am I alive at this time?

What does my presence bring that would not be here if I were not alive?

Does it matter who I am and what I do?

We are individuals *and* we are part of a whole—the whole of humanity. Just as each grain of sand makes up the beach and each drop of water makes up the ocean. All is one. This seems like a simple concept, and yet, it can be difficult for our finite minds to comprehend.

While brief in the timeline of all humanity, our individual journey does matter. Our existence does matter, and there is a purpose for our being alive, at this time.

Early in my EGE training, I was introduced to the ideas of Martha Graham and her philosophy on life and purpose. Her words resonated deep within me. She believed, as I do, that the energy that runs through us is our life force, and it is uniquely expressed by and through each individual. None of us is exactly the same. And the full authentic expression of this uniqueness is our gift to the world. If we hold back our expression, it will be lost, missing from the world. We are not to judge ourselves or compare ourselves to others. Our responsibility is to allow our expression to flow and "keep the channel open."[43]

Keeping the channel open means we do not allow our energy to become blocked or stuck, and if it does, we are tasked with finding a way to break free, to get our energy flowing again. I am convinced that blocked or stuck energy is the underlying cause for the majority of what ails us, including physical diseases and emotional disorders. Our health and our vitality have a direct relationship with how we manage our energy and how we relate to our life's purpose.

In 2010, I began to diligently study the concept of "life's purpose," which is also referred to as our "calling" or "God's will." It started with the urge I had to discover my own life's purpose and continued as I saw how integral it seemed to understanding the human condition and to finding ways to assist my clients toward their own break-throughs. It seemed like the quintessential puzzle piece necessary to have a satisfying life and to navigating change and transition. I became somewhat obsessed with it. I read many books on the topic that offered a variety of strategies and methods to help one discover life's purpose.

Up until the summer of 2017, I believed that the search for my life's purpose led me to an EGE program where I discovered my purpose is to be an EGE coach and facilitator. You would have read similar words on my website. Much of what I'd read and studied, up to that point, seemed to support the idea that each of us has "a" purpose—as in a singular purpose, one main purpose, *uno*, the one thing, the "*it*."

But then my perspective on the concept of life's purpose began to change. It started when I read the book *Designing Your Life* by Bill Burnett and Dave Evans. With each chapter, the authors suggested exercises in which one applies design principles to planning one's future, supplemented by examples of real-life client stories. As I read the clients' stories and I considered my own life, something clicked, or snapped really. I started to see multiple potential outcomes, all of which were exciting and desirable and "on purpose." There was no singular purpose. One's gifts, talents, and interests could be channeled into a myriad of different goals and activities. Their examples demonstrated the importance of being connected to the why behind a goal or activity and showed that not all goals and activities that one engages in need to have the same *why* or purpose.

As this idea of multiple potential outcomes permeated my thoughts, I began to see the pitfall of my previous philosophy around purpose. I felt the rigidity of the idea that we should have a singular purpose. In the midst of this contemplation, I came across something I'd written a few years before. It was part of my homework for a business development course. We were asked to write some belief statements about who we are, our goals, and our purpose.

I began to read it.

"God created me for *a* purpose. Each person is created for *a* purpose . . ."

The emphasis on the singular purpose made me cringe, and I was so repulsed, I couldn't even read the rest of it.

It was strange to remember the inspiration and connection I'd felt to those words as I wrote them, and then to feel the repulsion to those same words as I read them in that moment.

So, what changed?

At the time I read that document, I was not practicing EGE. I was on sabbatical from my work. The role I had played for several years had come to completion, and I had decided to take some time off before making any decision about how to move forward. According to what I had written, if I was not practicing EGE, then I was off my purpose. But that didn't feel right to me. I was taking a sabbatical "on purpose." I wanted to give myself the time and space to imagine the future without any lingering expectations based on the work I had been doing. What if I decided to pursue something new? What if I decided not to continue doing EGE? Who would I be if I weren't practicing EGE? According to this document, I wouldn't be me. Rubbish!

During my sabbatical, a major focus was helping my daughter select potential colleges. She was heading into her senior year of high school and would be starting the college application process in the fall. As part of this process, I had my daughter (and my 14-year-old son) take the Highlands Ability Battery, an assessment which measures a person's aptitudes, tendencies, the way they problem solve, the method and style of learning that comes naturally to them, and their inclinations and tolerances. These results were given differently than other assessments. For example, the assessment didn't list introvert on one side of the scale and extrovert on the other. There was one scale for introvert tendency and a separate scale for extrovert tendency.

The battery is based on the work of Johnson O'Connor, and over a century of research by O'Connor, himself, and the foundation bearing his name, Johnson O'Connor Research Foundation, has established that every individual is born with a pattern of abilities unique to him or her and that those abilities remain fairly stable after the age of fourteen.[44] One can learn new skills and tools, but if the person is re-tested years later, there is no significant fluctuation in assessment values. Their research has also shown that a person's overall satisfaction and happiness correlate directly with how much opportunity the person has to exercise their natural abilities in the course of their life, as opposed to how much the person is forced to operate in ways that are contrary. The reports we received with the results of the assessment battery listed a multitude of career options and courses of study that lined up with the particular combination of abilities for each of my children. I was amazed at the multiple potential opportunities listed for exercising their unique combinations of strengths.

A few months later, I had lunch with my friend, Mary, a professional intuitive coach. I always look forward to talking with Mary. There is a flow and a synchronicity that seem to emerge during our conversations, leaving me feeling inspired and energized. During lunch Mary shared about a recent women's circle she hosted where the group explored the topic of "life on purpose."

"Funny you should say that," I laughed.

And then I confessed to Mary my recent struggle with and dislike of the topic. It felt so awkward that this thing that I knew was so important, that I had felt so drawn to study, was now creating a strong resistance in me. I was feeling a little lost as I tried to examine my thought process. My conversation with her helped me realize that my understanding of the concept of "purpose" was expanding, and the resistance I felt to the topic was due to the conflict my new belief had with my old belief about a singular life's purpose. Both beliefs could not persist. One had to go.

Redefining my belief about purpose caused me to review an old contributor, the concept of "God's will." My view on this had also evolved over the years. When I was a little girl, the missionaries would come to speak in church about the work they were doing in other countries. In the church where I grew up, there was no greater calling, and the missionaries were revered for their commitment and sacrifice. They always held a prayer meeting where people would pray for each other to have the will of God revealed. On more than one occasion, I remember being terrified that God would call me to be a missionary, or that the thing I was supposed to do would be something I would dread. Back then I didn't know that God's will would never be something I would dread. I didn't have the understanding that the things I love, the things that inspire me, and the things I'm drawn to are there because that is how I was created. These things are of my soul, and they are the guideposts of my purpose.

During my process of redefining my belief about "life's purpose," I listened to a talk by Thomas Hübl, a spiritual teacher, and the key takeaways I received gave clarity to my new perspective, which closely resembles Martha Graham's quote. It helped me take the concept of life's purpose to the most basic universal level. Hübl spoke about energy awareness. He asked the questions *How vital do we feel? How is our life energy?*

If we get to the end of our day and we feel depleted, we need to examine where we were holding back, where we've dissociated, where our energy is blocked. The goal is to create an awake and present life where we live more and more out of our core intelligence (our unique expression), and we work on the unconscious areas and moments (where our energy gets blocked) in order to illuminate and address them (so we keep the channel open). **This is our life's purpose.**

If we need a holiday to recharge ourselves, something in our life is not working, and we need to examine where we are not living our life's purpose because we are allowing our energy to be blocked/stuck, and this is creating friction, resistance, and lowering our vitality. The more we step into our life's purpose (allowing our unique expression to flow), the more we will feel recharged by what we do.

My purpose is to be fully me, and your purpose is to be fully you, not what society or our families think we *should* be. If I don't do me, and you don't do you, then the world is missing something it is meant to have. We each have our own natural rhythm and energetic expression, and our purpose is for each of us to keep our energy flowing and expressing. The underlying, energetic basics are the same for all, but this will translate into action in different ways for each person, and there are multiple possibilities for each of us to fulfill our purpose.

Fate and Destiny

When we talk about purpose, the concepts of fate and destiny are not far behind. As I have just spoken about multiple possibilities and potential outcomes for your life, I want to clarify that I'm not saying there are infinite possibilities. The concept of infinite possibility is popular, and I see it being touted by some influential teachers and speakers. This idea is popular in the United States as we call ourselves "the land of possibility," and it gets reinforced by the "rags to riches" stories that we love to hear or read about.

The cosmic universe may contain the potential for infinite possibility, but our individual lives do not. In our lifetime, we do not have infinite possibilities, but in most cases, we have more possibilities and opportunities than we ever realize or acknowledge. The full range of these possibilities is our highest potential and our destiny. Our purpose is to pursue our destiny to its fullest within the boundaries of our fate.

What is fate? Fate has many facets. Fate is the culture and the time in history you were born into. Fate is your parents, your family, your DNA.

Fate in our DNA goes like this. Robert began gymnastics at a young age, and he was great at it. He was athletic and flexible and had excellent balance. He was on the path to Olympic level competition until he grew too tall. Fate is Robert surpassing the maximum height at which a gymnast can compete at the Olympic level. Robert's fate of not being able to pursue Olympic competition created a boundary that helped direct him toward his destiny of becoming a teacher, speaker, and author.

My friend's son, Ryan, wanted to be a navy fighter pilot, like Maverick in the movie *Top Gun*, but the Navy requires 20/20 vision for pilots, and Ryan's eye test revealed he doesn't have it. This is fate. Does that mean Ryan has to abandon his dream of flying for the Navy? No. Instead, he applied to be a weapons systems operator, the role of Goose in *Top Gun*, who sits behind the pilot advising him on radar, navigation, and tactical coordination.

The generations that came before influence the range of possibility that exists now for certain things connected to social and cultural consciousness. We can see fate's influence at the social and cultural levels through the success of Oprah Winfrey. Oprah's potential to be who she is came about because of the groundwork set by Martin Luther King, Jr., among others, and the movement he championed. If Oprah had been born prior to this movement, the possibility for her to develop into the person she is today would not have existed. The social changes we are making today will influence the fate and the potential of generations to come.

Before the invention of the telephone, if you wanted to communicate with someone outside of your town, you had to write a letter or travel yourself, and it would take days, weeks, or months to deliver your message. Today, we are not bound by that fate. I can send a text message or an email, and my friend in Maryland receives it almost instantaneously.

Time is also an element of fate. Gestation, germination, and lifespan are elements of fate, and we won't get far by fighting fate or feeling victimized by it. It is through the choices we make based on what is fated that we have the power to co-create our destiny, the highest potential for our life.

The archetypes of your personality and psyche are also part of your fate, and they serve your destiny. Two of my friends, who are also EGE colleagues, have a strong "rescuer" archetype. They both have a history of finding injured or abandoned animals, adopting them, and nursing them back to health. They are also driven to rescue people who are sick, hurt, or struggling in some way. If unchecked, the impulses of the rescuer can take over, and both of my friends have found themselves in situations where they are taking care of another (person or animal) to their own detriment.

It's no accident these two have the archetype of the rescuer. This archetype is common in people who are drawn to the healing arts and to animals, which is an element of destiny for both of them. By learning to manage their rescuer impulse, by discerning where and when to allow it, and making a conscious choice, these friends work with their fate to co-create their destiny.

Fate often has negative connotations. We see fate as restrictive or something bad that happens because it wasn't what we were hoping for in the moment. But it's really all about perspective. In some cases, after time has passed, we can reflect and see the bigger picture, and in it we can see how fate was working for us, or contributed to something that we now appreciate or even cherish.

In the summer of 1977, when I was five years old, my parents separated. My dad drove my mom, my sister and brother, and me from Costa Mesa, in Southern California, up north to live with my grandparents in San Jose. My parents' separation and eventual divorce had a huge impact on my life. It was a fated event that caused a lot of pain for all of us, but looking back, I know I would not be who I am today had I not experienced it.

Just as some experiences are fated, certain relationships are also fated and contribute to the boundary and context in which possibilities exist. Within weeks of our arrival in San Jose, my grandmother introduced my mom to a charismatic woman, Patricia Bigliardi, who lived in the same townhome complex and was also going through a marital separation/divorce. My mom and Pat quickly became friends, and I was introduced to Pat's nine-year-old son, Kelly. Later, I learned that Kelly was a nickname, and his real name was Achille. Meeting at the ages of five and nine was part of our fate, which held a potential for our destiny.

Achille and I had a childhood crush on each other that turned into a painful on-again, off-again relationship during high school. We had a lot of issues that created friction in our relationship, but we couldn't stay broken up. A year after I graduated Achille proposed. We were married on July 13, 1991, when I was nineteen, and he was twenty-three. Three years later, we divorced. A year later I remarried, and Kali was born in 1996. In early 1997, I woke up from a dream that was more of a vision and a spiritual intervention. I realized that the life I was living was not my life. I was way off course and I needed to find my way back.

At the time, Achille was engaged to someone else, and he also felt he was not on the right path. Eventually, we found our way back to each other, and we remarried on June 4, 1999. The things each of us learned about ourselves and life while we were apart were hard lessons, but I cherish them because they are precisely what have helped us stay together ever since.

When we follow it, destiny seems to give us little signposts and synchronicities that happen to let us know we are on the right track. Here is one such example. A couple of months after Achille and I were remarried, we decided that I would go off my birth control. We weren't trying to get pregnant, but we weren't preventing it either. Within two months, I was pregnant with Michaella and due the following July. Michaella arrived a few days before her due date on

July 13, 2000. Michaella's birthday is on the anniversary of our original wedding date. Every year when we celebrate Michaella's birthday, we also celebrate destiny. So much of who we are today has developed out of the good, the bad, the pain, and the joy of our relationship with each other, and we continue to grow as we face new phases of life together.

12

Bringing It to the Horse

The idea of getting advice from a horse isn't new. The television show *Mister Ed,* which first aired in 1961, about the talking horse that shared wisdom with his hapless owner, Wilbur, was inspired by short stories written in 1937 by Walter Brooks.[45]

Horses are archetypal, representing strength, courage, beauty, power, sensitivity, steadfastness, honesty, wisdom, and the list goes on. You'd be hard pressed to find a person who is not captivated by the sight of a swiftly moving horse. For multiple generations before the invention of the automobile, horses were a part of everyday life, whether you owned a horse or not. They were our partners in survival, with key roles in farming, ranching, transportation, and war.

In her book *The Power of The Herd: A Nonpredatory Approach to Social Intelligence, Leadership, and Innovation,* Linda Kohanov profiles cultural innovators who employed extraordinary leadership skills to change history, and they all had one thing in common. They were all accomplished equestrians: Winston Churchill, Alexander the Great, George Washington, Catherine the Great, Joan of Arc, General George Patton, and Siddhartha Gautama (the Buddha), among others. Winston Churchill is known for saying, "There is something about the outside of a horse that is good for the inside of a man." But this other, less well-known quote of his gives us a little more insight into his perspective. He said, "The substitution of the internal combustion engine for the horse marked a very gloomy milestone in the progress of mankind." Perhaps Churchill saw something of value in time spent around horses that went beyond accomplishing a day-to-day task or getting from point A to point B.

As horses have become less and less a part of daily life, their use has become more and more relegated to sport and entertainment. As urban areas expand, horse properties are being sold and developed for higher density housing and commercial use. Keeping a horse is becoming more difficult and more expensive, thus fewer and fewer people have access to horses. As a result multiple generations of city dwellers and others have grown up without horses in daily life and without the benefits of being around them.

Through her research of history's influential leaders, Kohanov points to a pattern that emerged in their stories. For thousands of years, the invisible forces of charisma, bravery, poise, focus, endurance, and conviction have been most reliably bolstered by a silent tutor (the horse). These qualities of influential leaders listed by Kohanov that came through riding, training, and time spent with horses are the same qualities we need to lead our own lives and to make powerful choices for meaningful change. If we can recognize the importance of the horse, not as a beast of burden or a companion, but as a teacher of kings, conquerors, heroes, and pioneers, surely we can see the value in becoming a student of the horse.[46]

Social Instinct

The main substrate for connection between humans and horses is the social instinct. Horses and humans are social animals, and we share similar social instincts. Horses are herd animals, and in order to survive in the wild, they need to be part of a herd, just like humans need to be part of our human herd, the group or community. Being alone or separated from the herd means certain death for both horse and human. Because of this herd instinct, horses are hardwired to relate to the other members of the herd, creating a social, hierarchical structure for coordination. This instinct in the horse creates a natural inclination for relationship and communication with humans.

A common misconception in some models of equine learning and therapy is that because the horse is a prey animal, there is a predator-prey relationship between humans and horses, with the human as the predator of the horse. I believe this misconception comes from equine activities based on certain horse training philosophies and methods like that of Monty Roberts and his Join-Up® technique.

Roberts studied wild mustangs and their movements and instincts. He learned that he could get a horse to trust him and come to him, what he calls "Join Up," by utilizing the horse's instinctual responses. Initially, he sends the horse away using predatory type movements. Then, when the horse gets tired of running away, and the horse is looking for other options, Roberts switches to movements and behaviors that are horse like, inviting the horse to join up or connect. The horse finds more comfort in being near Roberts than it does by continually trying to get away from him. While using a predatory movement may assist you in sending a horse away from you, it is not the only way to get a horse to move, and it does not mean you have a predator-prey relationship with the horse.

The predator-prey relationship is a specific biological relationship between two organisms of unlike species where one species is the hunted food source for the other. Examples of predator-prey relationships are the lion and zebra, bear and salmon, fox and rabbit. Horses and humans do not share in a predator-prey relationship.[47] But we can learn from their prey animal sensibilities.

Horse as Teacher

Unlike humans, a horse's default is to live in the present moment. As prey animals, their survival hinges on their ability to attune to their senses. Their systems are wired to go quickly into a survival response, and once a threat has passed, to quickly return to a balanced and relaxed state. In contrast, humans tend to prolong states of arousal by worrying about what to do or what we did. We relive a stressful scenario in our mind, holding on to the arousal and perpetuating its impact. We remain in higher states of stress far beyond what is necessary, causing damage to our health. Horses teach us a better way.

Horses are somatically integrated beings. When horses are not chronically confined to a stall and are given plenty of time outside and freedom to move around, they do not hold on to energy or energetic contractions. Horses will whinny, snort, toss their heads, fart, roll, buck, and rear as ways of expressing and moving energy through their bodies. Horses don't worry that their herd mates will judge them for such movements or for tending to their own needs.

This non-judgmental quality is an important factor in accepting the horse as our teacher, especially for people who have lost their trust in their fellow man due to deep wounds, trauma, spiritual abuse, or a long-time pattern of being and feeling judged. The horse doesn't care about how much money we make, what car we drive, or where we grew up, and the horse doesn't have an agenda. While in an EGE session, people feel that the horse sees into them and they trust the horse. Because of this, people are more open to the horse's feedback than that of another human. Those who have lost trust in people can establish trust with the horse, and through relationship with the horse, they find healing and a renewed ability to trust people.

When a we are near a horse, the wisdom of the body becomes more accessible than when we are sitting in chairs in a room. The horse connects to and responds to the energy of who we are being and how we are being in the moment, without labels, titles, or pretense. If we make a change in our body, our attitude, or our energy, the horse's response is immediate, helping us to zero in on our core topic or issue in minutes, rather than the weeks or months that it often takes in other coaching and therapy modalities. Being connected to the energy of the horse raises our awareness and accelerates the process of learning and change.

Horses reflect the energy of their environment, and that can include reflecting our energy back to us, helping us to see something we didn't see in ourselves or our situation (something unconscious). Often a horse will mirror the unproductive mood or attitude of a person, and when that person sees the impact of their mood or attitude on the horse, that the horse is at consequence for something inside of them, they become motivated to change, not for their own sake but for the horse's sake. This ability to reflect what's inside of us sometimes puts the horse in the role of the healer. When the horse's reflection offers validation of our energy or suppressed emotion, we feel seen, acknowledged, and understood. Horses can help us heal on an energetic/spiritual level through this connection.

When we are around horses, it usually means we are in a natural environment with less electricity, concrete, and mechanical influences. In urban settings, these influences bombard our bodies, causing a necessary desensitization. But when we are in a more natural environment, our sensitivity can return, allowing us to take in more information and listen more closely to our own internal messages.

Horse as Guide

Since prehistoric times, horses have been closely involved with humans, and until the early to mid-20th century, horses were part of day to day life, whether you owned a horse or not. Traveling into town to pick up your groceries you'd be riding a horse, driving a horse, or walking near and around horses. Based on the stories I've heard from hundreds of people, you'd be hard-pressed to find a person born before 1980 who didn't have an experience of being around a horse. It may have been unconscious, but if you ask someone about the experience, and they reflect back to it, they will note feeling something different, likely better, when they were in the presence of a horse.

There is no record of when horses became beneficial contributors to the lives of humans. But we can trace the beginning of the incorporation of horses into learning and healing models to the mid-1900s. In 1969, horses became part of physical therapy and rehabilitation with the founding of the North American Riding for the Handicapped Association (NARHA), later renamed PATH International. The physiological benefits of riding for the handicapped are well established. Because horseback riding rhythmically moves the rider's body in a manner similar to a human gait, riders with physical disabilities often show improvement in flexibility, balance, and muscle strength. As an activity, therapeutic riding contributes positively to the cognitive, physical, emotional, and social well-being of individuals with special needs, both physical and mental.[48] These programs are considered equine-assisted activities.

In the late 1980s and early 1990s, horses became involved with mental health and self-development. In 1989, Ariana Strozzi Mazzucchi, who later became my mentor, began incorporating horses into leadership training programs. As a lifelong horsewoman, Ariana knew the horses would give real-time feedback to her students who were practicing their leadership presence and coming into alignment with their goals. What Ariana didn't expect was that each and every person reported that the interaction they were having with the horse reflected exactly what was happening for them in their job, home life, relationship, etc.

Ariana invited her students to work with the horse as a metaphor for what was happening in their everyday life, and see if they could make a change. These early sessions created the groundwork for what she would later call Equine Guided Education.

The incorporation of horses into psychotherapy began in 1990 when Barbara K. Rector, M.A., implemented equine-facilitated psychotherapy at the Sierra Tucson treatment center, and later began her Adventures in Awareness programs, influencing current equine-facilitated activity models. Various forms of equine-assisted and equine-facilitated learning and therapy models continued to expand and evolve through the 1990s.

In 1999, after incorporating horses into self-development and leadership programs for ten years, Ariana coined the term Equine Guided Education. She carefully chose each word and assigned it a specific definition unique to the work:

Equine - A horse representing the ancient archetypes of strength, courage, dignity, power, honor, beauty, endurance, and resilience.

Guided - The magical ability of horses to take us into unknown or unexplored territory; a place where we can heal the past, reimagine our future, and connect to our life purpose and share our natural wisdom.

Education - Discipline of mind or character through study or instruction; dealing with the principles and practices of teaching and learning. Including educational, coaching, and therapeutic models that encourage effective relationship, communication, coordination, and social interaction skills for individuals and/or groups.[49]

Ariana found that the horses were not merely assisting or facilitating the process, they were actually guiding it. She learned that by directing her attention to follow the horse, and suggesting her students and clients also follow the attention of the horse, the reflection of the horse, or the energy reflected by the horse, everyone gained insights and clarity that had previously eluded them.

The value of the horse's guidance is not only relevant for the participant, but also for the facilitator. As a facilitator, it's easy to create our own interpretation of a client's situation, but to be an effective facilitator or coach, we must avoid projecting our own preferences, stories, or ideals onto the client's situation. My SkyHorseEGE™ training included getting to know myself, my own triggers, and my own preferences. This awareness helps me separate my "stuff" from what is happening with my client. If I have an idea of what's happening, and I'm following the horse, I will notice if my interpretation doesn't match the horse's reflection, and in that case, I know to let go of my interpretation and see what else is there.

Ariana felt the word education, based on her definition, encompassed the variety of models this work serves, and so far, it has served many. Between 2010 and 2017, I had the opportunity to work alongside Ariana in the SkyHorse Equine Guided Education certification program to train over one hundred students from within the United States and all over the world, including Spain, Italy, Switzerland, Canada, Netherlands, Turkey, Taiwan, Colombia, England, Australia, France, and Korea. The students came to learn how to incorporate horses into their own unique professional services, which include coaching, psychotherapy, art therapy, yoga, teaching, human resource development, organizational development, social work, horse training, riding instruction, and more.

By adding in the experiential component of horses, we accelerate the learning process, and we deepen the integration of what we have learned. When you engage in learning with a horse, your entire being becomes involved, not just your mind and intellect. The body becomes an active participant, and the spirit is activated through the energetic connection with the horse. When learning or an Aha! moment takes place, you have a visceral experience. It is not just a thought or mental concept, but it is felt throughout your entire being. This experience becomes a somatic marker, a feeling or sensation that you can return to later, even when the horse isn't present.

Heart of the Matter

For years there has been a lot of anecdotal evidence that people feel better when they are around horses. Participants who engage in equine supported educational activities report that when they addressed their issue or inquiry with the horse present, they discovered insights or clarity that had previously been inaccessible to them. As a facilitator, I've witnessed this with the students and participants I work with, and I've felt it for myself. In the past, I couldn't have said exactly *why* it was so, and I didn't feel the necessity to prove it. Knowing Equine Guided Education worked for people because I saw and felt it was good enough for me to keep doing it and trust it.

But recently, research has been done that seems to explain some of the how and the why that make EGE work. The research indicates that the heart of the horse plays a key role in the effectiveness of equine coaching, learning, and therapy models.

First, let's look at the human heart. The human heart generates the largest electromagnetic field in the body. The magnetic field produced by the heart is more than 100 times greater in strength than that of the brain, and this field can be detected and measured three feet away, in all directions from a person's body, and between two individuals in close proximity.[50] The average human heart weighs less than one pound, while the average horse heart weighs between nine and eleven pounds. Highly athletic horses have been found to have larger than average hearts. Secretariat's heart was twenty-two pounds. The horse's larger heart generates an electromagnetic field that is five times greater than the human one.

According to a HeartMath study when people touch or are in close proximity, there's a transference of the electromagnetic energy produced by the heart and encoded within it is subtle energetic communication beyond what's typically considered non-verbal communication, i.e. facial expression, tone of voice, and body language. This electromagnetic or "energetic" communication operates at a subconscious level via the nervous system, which acts as an antenna, tuning into the magnetic field produced by the hearts of other people (and animals).[51] This transference of subtle energetic information occurring between the magnetic field of a human and horse helps to explain how a horse is able to detect subtle feelings, moods, and energetic shifts, and reflect them back to the participant in an EGE session.

Horses living in natural, non-stressful environments are likely to spend most of their time in balanced states characterized as *coherent*. As it relates to the heart, coherence refers to a state characterized by harmony, stability, synchronization, and efficient or optimal function. While functioning in a coherent mode, the heart pulls other biological systems into synchronization, leading to entrainment, a state with increased coherence between each system. The coherent state correlates to improvements in cognitive function, and social and physical performance, and a general sense of well-being.[52]

With the horse's magnetic field being stronger than that of a human, it is not difficult to see how a horse in a coherent state can influence the humans in their proximity into a more coherent state, and it is not surprising that many people report "feeling better" when they are around horses. This may also explain why a person can get to the "heart of the matter" more quickly when they are in the presence of a horse. With the horse's state contributing to coherence in the human and entrainment of the human's heart and brain, they are better able to find alignment between what the heart wants and what the brain thinks. This state is more conducive to integrating new information and perspectives, and finding clarity.

It is from a state of coherence that we are best able to access our internal guidance system, increasing our ability to move beyond habitual reactions and perceptions, and to better access our inner wisdom and intuitive discernment. With practice, we can learn to more easily make self-directed, heart-centered choices through a connection to our internal guidance system.

It may not only be the energetics of the horse's heart that influence the effectiveness of EGE. There is also something interesting about the physical alignment of our heart space with a horse's heart space when we interact with them.

If an average-sized person stands next to an average-sized horse, the two hearts line up on the same horizontal plane. And when we sit on a horse's back to ride, our hearts share the same vertical plane. Time and time again, when I have been working with a client, and that client begins to speak from their heart, the horse will walk over and align its heart space to the person's heart. With no agenda or judgment, this response by the horse has given many people the affirmation and confirmation they needed to trust what their hearts wanted.

A Uniquely Integrated Approach

Equine Guided Education, as it relates to human development, is the basis of my work. Through years of studying the principles and practicing EGE, I have integrated it deeply into my everyday life and how I work with clients, even when I don't have a horse present. Because each person is unique, no singular system or method is sufficient, and I can't always have a horse with me so it has been necessary to develop additional tools and methods.

When I work with my clients, I listen to their stories. I listen for beliefs and fears, and I take note of what repeats. I pay attention to what they are focused on, what does or doesn't have energy in their story, how they interpret what is happening for them, repetitive phrases, or attitudes and habits. I note if their body language is or is not congruent with their words. I watch to see how the horse responds to them, to what they are saying. All of these give clues to what might be going on that we can further explore. The additional tools and methods I choose to use at any given time depend on the specifics of the client's situation and needs.

In addition to the method of EGE, I incorporate the wisdom gained from my own life lessons and a variety of complementary philosophies, tools, and methods. Tools and methods derived from psychology and somatics provide certain language and practices that are useful in addressing the mind and body, but these languages alone are not sufficient to address the spirit and soul. EGE provides language to address the spirit, and the language and articulation provided by the use of archetypes, myths, and metaphors expand on it to include the soul.

CONCLUSION

I hope that somewhere in these pages you have found an insight or an Aha! that leads you to freedom, to break free of the beliefs, patterns, fears, and habits that might be holding you back, preventing you from living a satisfying life. Flow and satisfaction come through alignment with your internal guidance system and the pursuit of your soul's destiny. I encourage you to take up the reins and lead yourself into your future. Make a commitment to be you. Begin now.

THE NEXT STEP

Getting unstuck requires action.
Take the next step with my
What's Your Story? - journaling exercise.
It's available free as my gift to you.

To download, go to
www.halliebigliardi.com/whatsyourstory.

For information on upcoming workshops
or a private session, or to connect with me,
please visit *www.halliebigliardi.com.*

ACKNOWLEDGMENTS

There are two distinct areas of gratitude that I wish to acknowledge. I am grateful to the many people who contributed to my education and work experience that form the basis of this book, for without them I would not have this content to share, and I'm grateful to a small but mighty band of folks who are the ones that helped me get the words on the page and this book in tangible form.

I'll start with the book. Without the contribution of my husband, Achille Bigliardi IV, and my writing coach, Robin Colucci, this book would not exist. Over the years, many people said to me that I should write a book. My husband, Achille, was the most persistent among them. Each time someone made the suggestion, I would respond with an "Oh, thanks, it's nice of you to say that, but it's not going to happen." I appreciated their suggestion because, underneath, it was as if they were also saying "You have valuable insights that are worthy of being published." But I never had any desire to write a book. Writing has always been a painstaking process for me. I edit myself before I even finish typing a sentence, and I can spend hours on a two-paragraph email. I knew writing a book would take extreme commitment and a strong desire, which I did not have.

In the fall of 2017, during my sabbatical, my husband, Achille, brought up the book idea again. This time there was a sureness in his voice that I had not heard or felt before. This time he meant I should do it now. My first task was to look for guidance on *how* to write a book. So I searched online and that's how I discovered Robin Colucci's book *How to Write a Book That Sells You.*

I ended up doing a two-day intensive with her to map out my concept and outline, and then hired her to help me write it. Through-out the process, Robin guided me step by step and she taught me the tools I was lacking. As I learned from her, the writing process got easier and easier. The combination of accountability, support, encouragement, and mentorship that came from Robin was invaluable to me during this process.

Achille supported me the whole way through. He completely honored my writing time. It became my work, my job to be writing. On days that I had a deadline, he would make dinner and take over the coordination of our children's schedules. There were times I was not so fun to be around, and he had to spend several evenings without my companionship as I kept to my rigorous schedule. He is my best friend, soulmate, and the love of my life. For forty-one years, we have been each other's training partner through some of the toughest life lessons, but the challenges and difficulties, pain and hurts, could not keep us apart. He is my rock, my confidant, and my foundation of support. His sense of humor and silly anecdotes bring laughter that helps to break up the seriousness that at times befalls my mode of thinking. He is a part of everything that is valuable and precious to me. His love and encouragement give me the strength and courage to put myself out there and reach for my dreams.

Another key supporter in making the book happen was my dear friend and colleague, Cameron Ashley Smith. Our friendship began in our SkyHorseEGE™ certification course, and since then, we have co-facilitated many programs together. Ashley was my confidant throughout the entire book writing process. She gave me her full support and encouragement. Ashley was the only person other than Robin to read my manuscript before it was finished. Ashley's enthusiasm for my first few chapters helped to fuel my confidence to press on and work through the sticky places and frustrations, and I am deeply grateful for her support and friendship.

Special thanks go to my daughter Michaella and my son, Achille, for honoring the importance of my book project and never once complaining to me about the limits it placed on my availability for them. Often both would ask me how it was going and how I was doing, and they were conscientious listeners whether my response was one of frustration or excitement. Several times Michaella sat with me and listened as I read through parts that I was struggling with, and she would offer her suggestions and support. I am grateful for each of my children, Michaella, Achille, and my firstborn, Kali. The unique presence of who they are as individuals and who they are becoming as they grow makes it an honor to be their mother and to participate in their amazing lives.

To my friends at the barn, Wednesday Dull, Katie Marzullo, Barbara Smith, Kelly Sayer, Roberta Clift, Jolie Veltmann, Ursula Murray, Jessica Fischer, and Steve Fuqua, thanks for cheering me on and supporting me. Your encouragement, especially on those tough days, was greatly appreciated.

And thanks to Robin Parker Meredith, who met me on that summer day in a Los Gatos park, for the suggestions and encourage-ment that became seeds for writing the book and helped to inform the voice and content.

Thank you to my friend, colleague, and fellow solution wrangler, Amanda Kent, for her support and encouragement, and for celebrating with me at the completion of my first draft.

The fact that I had the basic skills to write and avert driving my writing coach crazy brings me to thank my elementary school teacher, Mrs. Tennie Reynolds, for setting the foundation through drills and practice.

Thanks and gratitude go to my production team: Polly Letofsky, Lucia Brown, and Nick Zelinger. Thank you for your expertise and excellent work. I could not be happier with the finished product and my experience of the process.

I'd like to thank everyone who ever said to me "You should write a book," and to everyone who offered me encouraging words and support during the process.

The education and experience that form the basis of this book have come through an accumulation of the lessons learned through my entire life to this point, and I am grateful to everyone I have met and interacted with and all the experiences that have contributed to my learning. There are some key individuals I would like to thank specifically.

The foundational aspect of this book is Equine Guided Education, and I would first like to express my gratitude, which goes beyond what I can convey with words, to Ariana Strozzi Mazzucchi for developing the work of Equine Guided Education. I am grateful for her pioneering efforts in the field of the horse as healer/teacher, for the generosity with which she taught and shared the jewels of her discoveries, for her years of dedication to teaching her students, and for her ongoing stewardship of Mother Earth and her creatures. From my first day in her class, I felt privileged to have the opportunity to learn from her, and later, I was honored to be chosen as a mentee and someone she would train to teach other people. Thanks to Ariana for sharing the gift of EGE, for being my teacher and mentor, and becoming my friend. The work she brought forward changed my life and the lives of so many others for the better. I would not be who I am today without her influence.

A special thank you goes to Nancy Harrington for introducing me to Ariana's work and for being a friend and confidant throughout my EGE learning process.

Another significant contributor to the person I am today is Coach J Shoop. Through weekly calls over the course of seven years, Coach Shoop offered his compassionate guidance, intuitive insights, and supportive wisdom. His coaching provided many tools for self-discovery, changing unproductive mindsets, and accomplishing goals. His mentorship during that key transformational period was crucial to my success. His commitment to me and my success was invaluable, and his belief in me helped me to believe in myself. I am forever grateful to Coach Shoop for his dedication, encouragement, and guidance.

I also want to thank two people whose work has had a great influence on my own. First, Caroline Myss whose teaching on archetypes and Sacred Contracts gave me a new lens with which to view myself and helped me to further become who I am meant to be. Through the practice of my own contract, I have been able to help others do the same. Her brilliant work has provided me the language, structure, and understanding to articulate the things I see in people that keep them stuck and can help get them unstuck.

The Intuitive-Archetypal Astrology work of Robert Ohotto has also informed my work and given me the roadmap to understanding the cycles of human development. His symbolic sight and the method of interpretation he models have helped me to better understand myself and my soul contract. Through the lens his teaching provides, I have more clarity about where I am going, and I am better able to facilitate my clients in their process of discovery.

Special thanks to all my colleagues with whom I have co-facilitated, studied, and practiced, and all those who have staffed with me in EGE programs learning side by side.

Thank you to the students of SkyHorseEGE™ and other program participants who gave me the opportunity to learn, grow, practice, share, and teach.

Thank you to all of my clients who have trusted me and the horses with the important subject matter of their lives and relationships.

Deep appreciation and gratitude go to my long-time riding instructor and friend, Diana Disney, for teaching me almost everything

I know about riding and horse care. Thanks to Cevalo Riding Academy for allowing me to hold my first EGE workshop with your horses. And thanks to Sandy Anderson and Bob Hughes of Valley View Ranch for overseeing the care of my horse, and for allowing me to rent space for workshops and client sessions.

Thanks to my mom and dad for always supporting me in everything I do. Your love has been present for me throughout my entire life, especially during my dark and challenging years. I appreciate you both for the values you've taught me and for consistently being there when I need you most.

To my late mother-in-law, author Patricia Bigliardi, thank you for your belief in me and my EGE work. I know how excited you would have been for me to write a book, and I imagine you looking down with pride.

Thanks to my father-in-law, Achille Bigliardi III, for advising and mentoring me in business matters, and to him and his wife, Kim, for their overall encouragement, support, and love.

To my brothers, Geoffrey and Kevin Helton, and my sister, Theresa Moser, thank you for loving and supporting me through good times and tough times. I am grateful to have siblings with whom I get along and can be myself and share what's important to me.

Thanks to my brothers- and sisters-in-law: Heidi Lidtke, Teri Helton, Matt Moser, and Matt and Kirsten Bigliardi, and to my extended family of aunts, uncles, and cousins for your love, support, and influence on my life over the years. And an extra thank you to my aunt, Claire Pfann, and my cousins, Shoshie Pfann and Missy Takano, for your consultation on some of the Greek and Hebrew meanings used in this book.

Also, thanks to the friends who supported me and the friends who supported Achille while he was supporting me, not only through the process of the book, but throughout our lives together:

Tony and Renee Fini, Andree Braun, Mike Wilson, Jordan Reeder, Steve Severino, James and Katie Gutierrez, Kelli Rivers, and all of Achille's gym buddies.

Finally, to all my equine mentors and partners, past, present and future, with special mention to my horse Cari, and to Lacy, Sadie, Lottie, and the rest of the SkyHorse herd, thank you for your generosity of spirit, your wisdom, resilience, and honesty, and the opportunity to experience the bliss of our genuine connection. Thank you for teaching and guiding me and the clients we serve together. Thank you for recognizing when someone needs healing before they can receive teaching. Thank you for the magic your presence offers and for the awe you inspire in me through every EGE moment.

ABOUT THE AUTHOR

Hallie Bigliardi facilitates and coaches individual EGE sessions and group workshops using her uniquely integrated approach, which honors the interconnected aspects of body, mind, spirit, and soul, to address the challenges we all face in the process of human development and life. Through Hallie's personal and professional experiences and continuing education, she has become an expert in the areas of relationships, authentic communication, and facilitating transformational breakthroughs.

In 2010, Hallie completed the SkyHorseEGE™ certification program. Under the instruction and mentorship of Ariana Strozzi Mazzucchi, founder of SkyhorseEGE™, Hallie spent the next eight years developing her skills as a facilitator and coach by staffing and teaching for SkyHorseEGE™ programs, while simultaneously becoming an instructor in the SkyHorseEGE™ certification program, helping to certify hundreds of people from all over the world in the work of EGE. Hallie Bigliardi is a Level Five Certified SkyHorseEGE™ Coach and Instructor.

In addition to the principles of SkyHorseEGE™, Hallie draws from her extensive study of human development themes through the lens of archetypes from Caroline Myss' Sacred Contracts course, as well as the Intuitive-Archetypal Astrology work in Robert Ohotto's Soul Destinies course. With these added dimensions and perspective, Hallie bridges the practices of somatics and the body-mind-spirit concept with the themes and language of the soul. By combining complementary aspects of these philosophies and methods with Equine Guided Education, Hallie has developed a uniquely integrated approach for getting unstuck and moving forward toward meaningful change.

Hallie is a guest lecturer for students of the Equine Science program at Colorado State University, helping to further their learning of equine behavior and the benefits of horse-human interaction. Hallie lives in San Jose, California, with her husband, children, horse, and two dogs.

NOTES

[1] Used by permission from Lynne Twist, www.soulofmoney.org.

[2] "Self Storage Industry Statistics – Statistic Brain," *Statistic Brain Research Institute*, September 4, 2016, https://www.statisticbrain.com/self-storage-industry-statistics/.

[3] Harold Pashler, Mark McDaniel, Doug Rohrer, and Robert A. Bjork, "Learning Styles: Concepts and Evidence," *Psychological Science in the Public Interest* 9 no. 3 (December 2009): 117, http://journals.sagepub.com/doi/10.1111/j.1539-6053.2009.01038.x/.

[4] David Glenn, "Matching Teaching Style to Learning Style May Not Help Students," *The Chronicle of Higher Education*, December 15, 2009, https://www.chronicle.com/article/Matching-Teaching-Style-to/49497.

[5] Olivia Goldhill, "The Concept of Different 'Learning Styles' Is One of the Greatest Neuroscience Myths," *Quartz*, January 3, 2016, https://qz.com/585143/the-concept-of-different-learning-styles-is-one-of-the-greatest-neuroscience-myths/; Derek Bruff, "Learning Styles: Fact and Fiction – A Conference Report," *Vanderbilt University Center for Teaching*, January 28, 2011, https://cft.vanderbilt.edu/2011/01/learning-styles-fact-and-fiction-a-conference-report/.

[6] Maryellen Weimer, "What's the Story on Learning Styles?," *Faculty Focus* (blog), *The Teaching Professor Blog*, April 30, 2014, https://www.facultyfocus.com/articles/teaching-professor-blog/whats-story-learning-styles/.

[7] Pat Burke Guild, "Diversity, Learning Style and Culture," *New Horizons for Learning*, accessed January 31, 2018, http://archive.education.jhu.edu/PD/newhorizons/strategies/topics/Learning%20Styles/diversity.html.

[8] Alec Julian, "Dualism in the Movies," *We Love Philosophy* (blog), March 20, 2013, https://welovephilosophy.com/2013/03/20/dualism-in-the-movies/.

[9] "Wikipedia: Psychology," Wikimedia Foundation, last modified May 20, 2018, https://en.wikipedia.org/wiki/Psychology.

[10] Neil R. Carlson et al., *Psychology: the Science of Behavior 7th Edition* (New York: Pearson Education Inc., 2010), 18.

[11] *Introduction to Psychology, "1.2 The Evolution of Psychology: History, Approaches, and Questions," Figure 1.5,* University of Minnesota Libraries Publishing edition, 2015, chap. 1, http://open.lib.umn.edu/intropsyc/chapter/1-2-the-evolution-of-psychology-history-approaches-and-questions/.

[12] E. J. Mundell, "Antidepressant Use Jumps 65 Percent in 15 Years," *HealthDay via WebMD,* August 15, 2017, https://www.webmd.com/depression/news/20170815/us-antidepressant-use-jumps-65-percent-in-15-years#1.

[13] Brendan L. Smith, "Inappropriate Prescribing," *American Psychological Association* 43, no. 6, (June 2012), http://www.apa.org/monitor/2012/06/prescribing.aspx.

[14] Olivia Goldhill, "Scientists Say Your 'Mind' Isn't Confined to Your Brain, or Even Your Body," *Quartz*, December 24, 2016, https://qz.com/866352/scientists-say-your-mind-isnt-confined-to-your-brain-or-even-your-body/.

[15] Jeff Thompson, "Is Nonverbal Communication a Numbers Game?," *Psychology Today*, September 30, 2011, https://www.psychologytoday.com/blog/beyond-words/201109/is-non-verbal-communication-numbers-game.

[16] "Human Brain – Neuroscience – Cognitive Science," *Basic Knowledge 101*, accessed May 8, 2018, http://www.basicknowledge101.com/subjects/brain.html.

[17] A key distinction taught by Ariana Strozzi Mazzucchi during the SkyHorseEGE™ training.

[18] Adam Hadhazy, "Think Twice: How the Gut's 'Second Brain' Influences Mood and Well-Being," *Scientific American*, February 12, 2010, https://www.scientificamerican.com/article/gut-second-brain/.

[19] Center for Somatic Studies' "Developmental Somatic Psychotherapy Definitions" entry, accessed May 8, 2018, https://somaticstudies.com/developmental-somatic-psychotherapy/definitions/.

[20] Ariel Giarretto, "Healing Trauma Through the Body: The Way In Is the Way Out," *Psychotherapy.net*, 2010, https://www.psychotherapy.net/article/healing-trauma-somatic.

[21] Ariana Strozzi Mazzucchi, *Equine Guided Education: Horses Healing Humans Healing Earth* (CreateSpace Independent Publishing Platform, 2015), 135.

[22] Book of James, chapter two, verse twenty-six, *The New American Standard Bible*, (La Habra, CA: The Lockman Foundation, 1977).

[23] Book of Proverbs, chapter eighteen, verse fourteen, *The Holy Bible*, New Living Translation, (Wheaton, IL: Tyndale House Publishers, Inc., 1996, 2004).

[24] "Wikipedia; Shinto" Wikimedia Foundation, last modified June 3, 2018, https://en.wikipedia.org/wiki/Shinto.

[25] "Wikipedia; Qi" Wikimedia Foundation, last modified May 23, 2018, https://en.wikipedia.org/wiki/Qi.

[26] David Frawley, "Understanding Prana," *Yoga International*, accessed February 15, 2018, https://yogainternational.com/article/view/understanding-prana.

[27] "Difference Between Soul and Spirit," *Difference Between/Descriptive Analysis and Comparisons*, accessed May 8, 2018, http://www.difference-between.info/difference-between-soul-and-spirit.

[28] "Wikipedia; Soul" Wikimedia Foundation, last modified May 18, 2018, https://en.wikipedia.org/wiki/Soul.

[29] Ibid.

[30] "Karma" from the Yogic Encyclopedia," *Ananda Sangha* Worldwide, accessed May 8, 2018, https://www.ananda.org/yogapedia/karma/.

[31] Caroline Myss, "The Basis of Sacred Contracts," *Caroline Myss* (website), accessed March 8, 2018, https://www.myss.com/free-resources/sacred-contracts-and-your-archetypes/the-basis-of-sacred-contracts/.

[32] Michael Lipka and Claire Gecewicz, "More Americans Now Say They're Spiritual but Not Religious," *Pew Research Center*, September 6, 2017, http://www.pewresearch.org/fact-tank/2017/09/06/more-americans-now-say-theyre-spiritual-but-not-religious/.

[33] Heather Tomlinson, "Spiritual Abuse," *Premier Christianity,* September 2010, https://www.premierchristianity.com/Past-Issues/2010/September-2010/Spiritual-Abuse.

[34] Andrea Matthews, "Therapy and Spiritual Abuse," *Psychology Today,* April 5, 2016, https://www.psychologytoday.com/blog/traversing-the-inner-terrain/201604/therapy-and-spiritual-abuse.

[35] Anne Solomon, "Spirituality & Religion," *Anne Solomon* (website), January 30, 2017, https://www.spiritual-life.co.uk/single-post/ 2017/01/ 30/Spirituality-Religion.

[36] Sid Jefries, "Astrology and Religion: One World, One God, Many Names, Many Faces," *Facts Behind Faith*, accessed May 8, 2018, http://www.factsbehindfaith.com/default.aspx?intContentID=33.

[37] Robert Ohotto, "Intuitive- Archetypal Astrology," *Robert Ohotto Intuitive Astrologer* (website), accessed March 8, 2018, http://ohotto.com/features/intuitive_archetypal_astrology.asp.

[38] Polly LaBarre, "Do You Have the Will to Lead?," *Fast Company,* February 29, 2000, https://www.fastcompany.com/38853/do-you-have-will-lead.

[39] Ibid.

[40] Tony Schwartz, *The Way We're Working Isn't Working* (New York: Free Press, 2011).

[41] Caroline Myss, C. Norman Shealy, *The Creation of Health* (New York: Three Rivers Press, 1988, 1993).

[42] Jack P. Shonkoff and Andrew S. Garner, "The Lifelong Effects of Early Childhood Adversity and Toxic Stress," Abstract. *American Academy of Pediatrics*, 2012, http://pediatrics.aappublications.org/content/129/1/e232.

[43] Agnes De Mille, *Martha: The Life and Work of Martha Graham* (New York: Random House, 1991), 264.

[44] "The History of the HAB," *The Highlands Company* (website), accessed March 25, 2018, https://www.highlandsco.com/whats-highlands-ability-battery/hab-technology-and-research/.

[45] "Horse Around with These 14 Fascinating Facts about 'Mister Ed'," *MeTV* (website), July 29, 2016, https://www.metv.com/lists/horse-around-with-these-14-fascinating-facts-about-mister-ed.

[46] Linda Kohanov, T*he Power of the Herd* (Novato, CA: New World Library, 2013), 226.

[47] *Encyclopedia.com*, s.v. "Predator-Prey Relationships," accessed May 8, 2018, https://www.encyclopedia.com/environment/energy-government-and-defense-magazines/predator-prey-relationships.

[48] "Learn About EAAT/Learn About Therapeutic Riding," *PATH International* (website), accessed May 8, 2018, https://www.pathintl.org/resources-education/resources/eaat/198-learn-about-therapeutic-riding.

[49] Ariana Strozzi Mazzucchi, *Equine Guided Education: Horses Healing Humans Healing Earth* (CreateSpace Independent Publishing Platform, 2015), 20.

[50] McCraty, Rollin, *Science of the Heart, Exploring the Role of the Heart in Human Performance Volume 2*, HeartMath® Institute, 2015, 36, www.heartmath.org.

[51] McCraty, Rollin, *Science of the Heart, Exploring the Role of the Heart in Human Performance Volume 2*, HeartMath® Institute, 2015, 38-39, www.heartmath.org.

[52] McCraty, Rollin, *Science of the Heart, Exploring the Role of the Heart in Human Performance Volume 2*, HeartMath® Institute, 2015, 24-26, www.heartmath.org.